# RIPTIDE
The
NEW NORMAL
for
HIGHER EDUCATION

**DAN ANGEL and TERRY CONNELLY**

ISBN # 978-0-9835095-2-3

Library of Congress Control Number: 2011927973




Published by The Publishing Place
Ashland, KY
www.thePubPlace.com

"There is a tide in the affairs of men.
Which, taken at the flood, leads on to fortune:
Omitted, all the voyage of their life
Is bound in shallows and in miseries.
On such a full sea are we now afloat,
And we must take the current when it serves,
Or lose our ventures."
                    Shakespeare
                    Julius Caesar

# Foreword

Dan Angel and Terry Connelly have pooled their considerable experience and insights in higher education and high finance to provide a unique, outside-in, three-dimensional probe into the complex, confusing, and convoluted world of higher education.

As proven change agents, they put their fingers precisely on the pulse of our times to identify the converging forces that beg for change in our aging and unresponsive university model: the Great Recession, Graduation Gridlock, competition from abroad, the power of online, the rise of the for-profit universities, multi-generational concerns, and much more.

Mixing direct, personal experiences in business, politics, and higher education against a backdrop of individual and at-large societal needs, they pinpoint how and why American higher education has lost its edge: failing to provide a cost-effective path to degree completion for the 85 percent of today's students who don't fit the traditional model, and thereby robbing our nation of the talent needed to maintain our economic standing and our standard of living.

The pair then present a clear, simple and focused plan of action to allow colleges to live within their financial means and save the American taxpayer real money, while delivering on America's three "A-word" higher education needs: access, affordability and attainment.

Angel and Connelly pack quite a wallop with their fresh and feisty, no-holds-barred commentary on the continual "talk, talk, talk" that surrounds, retards and inhibits meaningful, broad-based higher-education reform.

From a RIPTIDE sense of urgency, we are urged to TOUCH THE THIRD RAIL and go far beyond the usual cosmetic and routine to embrace a new THREE-YEAR NO FRILL PUBLIC OPTION that fully delivers on our country's promise of educational opportunity.

Their case is compelling.

If you're looking for clarity in the current quagmire of American higher education, you will be both surprised and delighted by the bold approach and action plan proposed in these pages.

Les Schmidt, CEO
SONGBIRD
San Francisco

# TABLE OF CONTENTS

# RIPTIDE

"Why should colleges be immune to the
changes sweeping just about every other
industry in the country?"
Brian Kelly, Editor
*US News & World Report*

A few years ago, on a fundraising visit in my capacity as president of
Marshall University, I made a memorable stop in California. We were
picked up in a black, stretch limousine and whisked off toward Malibu
Beach.

As we left the narrow and crowded highway, a private gate parted
revealing a breathtaking home that backed up to the ocean. On the sec-
ond-floor balcony, we sipped wine and sampled cheese in the warm, late-
afternoon sunlight as the tide began to come in. Rushing ever-closer to the
shore it began to extend to the area just beneath our balcony. Our host
indicated that if we wanted to walk on the beach, we would need to do so
before the tide fully came in.

As we paused at the lower staircase to the beach, our host cautioned
that the ocean tide could be exceedingly strong. He suggested that at the
right moment, we quickly jog to the halfway point, step back ten yards
onto the steps there and wait for the tide to recede before proceeding.

Being from the Midwest, standing six-foot-four, and having my fair share of macho, I decided that I would skip the "halfway" nonsense and jog the full distance.

That was a mistake! The force of the tide threw me like a rag doll into the side of the beach wall. But that was not the worst part: As rapidly as I hit the wall, I was pulled with intense force toward the sea. The water was cold and much more salty than I had imagined. Five yards. Ten yards. It occurred to me that I might be a goner.

Finally, the ocean did release me. I lay there momentarily dazed. My sunglasses, hat and thongs were afloat somewhere "out there" and I made no effort to reclaim them. I had been surprised, unprepared and humbled by what had happened.

My wife Patricia still kids with me about "My Malibu Riptide Experience."

But now four years into the Great Recession of 2007, there are many similarities between the gripping force that toppled me then and the mega-forces that are now entrapping our national economy and our higher education system along with it.

With a ferocity not experienced since the Great Depression, we were hit by a tsunami-force riptide that has changed everything. According to a Crisis Impact Poll of November 2009, 70 percent of Americans experienced a job loss or a pay cut, or knew someone who had. Two-thirds of the respondents could not believe that "America was in this mess." The poll concluded that the nation's spending habits, relationships, hopes and attitudes toward Wall Street, the government, and many trusted institutions were profoundly shaken. In July 2010, an economic survey by *USA Today* found that 79 percent of the participating experts were "less optimistic" than they'd been just three months earlier.

Make no mistake about the extent of the damage. *Bloomberg* relates a stunning and breathtaking statistic: "The world's largest economy shrank 4.1 percent from the fourth quarter of 2007 to the second quarter of

2009."

More than 8 million jobs have been lost since December 2007, and the Labor Department estimates than half will not be coming back. In August 2010, more than 14 million Americans were without work. Unemployment rose in 30 states at the start of the year and by midyear 2010 the national unemployment rate still hovered in the 10 percent range. First-time jobless monthly claims reached 650,000 in March 2009, but were still at 500,000 in July 2010. By November 2010 fully one quarter of the national workforce was either unemployed or underemployed.

A poll of recruiting officers in spring 2010 indicated that 73 percent of the companies did not plan to hire before the end of year. Federal Reserve Chairman Ben Bernanke predicted that, by December 2011, unemployment would be no better than 7.5 percent. The consensus of the *USA Today* economic report was that we will not regain the 8 million jobs lost "until 2015 or later." Amazingly, nearly half (47 percent) of our nation's individuals and households earned so little income in 2009 that they paid no federal income tax, according to the Tax Policy Center.

Moody's chief economist Mark Zandi estimates that 400,000 local and state employees could lose their jobs in FY 2010 because of shrinking public tax coffers. That number would double the 200,000 jettisoned in the 2009 fiscal year. State budgets have weathered a quarter-trillion-dollar deficit over the past two years.

In July 2010 the Employee Benefit Research Institute speculated that many Americans would not have enough to pay for their likely span of retirement years. In 2005 one in four senior citizens planned to work past age sixty-five; by 2010, that number had grown to one in three. Today one in seven Americans lives in poverty, one in eight receives food stamps (an increase from 28 million to 40 million since December 2007), and one in six (more than 50 million) are without health insurance.

Adding insult to injury, those fortunate enough to be working pay more for their health care. Average workers saw their share of insurance premiums rise by 14 percent in September 2010, according to the Kaiser Family Foundation and Health Research and Educational Trust. Workers also pay higher deductibles, typically $1,000.

On the housing front, for the first time since 1945 (when data began to be recorded) the total debt of American homeowners was more than aggregate homeowner equity. Sales of new homes dropped like lead balloons after the $8,000 first-time-buyer and $6,500 repeat-buyer tax credits ended on April 30. Realty Trade Inc.'s statistical trend lines show that the rate of foreclosures will likely top the 900,000 homes repossessed in 2009. Indeed, US Census workers found 14 million homes unoccupied in 2010, up a full 50 percent over the 2000 census. The surge in foreclosures pushed home ownership back to 1999 levels.

The stock market has been more ghoulish than bearish. In spite of recording average returns approaching 10 percent since 1926, the average gain over the past decade has been less that 0.5 percent. During the first six months of 2010 the Dow Jones Industrial Average fluctuated more than 1,500 points but showed no gain whatsoever for the year.

Household income took a beating in 2008, dropping almost 4 percent in just one year. Bankruptcies have tripled since 2006. General Motors sold more cars in China last year than in the US. The poverty rate grew to 13 percent in 2008. It's enough to drive you postal.

Meanwhile, Medicare recipients increased by 3 million over the past three years while Medicaid and its related Children's Health Insurance Program grew by 7 million over the same thirty-six months. Today those programs cover 106 million Americans—(one in three of us).

Federal stimulus funds are petering out and there is little taxpayer tolerance for extending them. The number of bank failures doubled in the first half of 2010. More than a quarter of voting-age Americans has Tea

Party leanings. The federal 2011 budget recorded a $1 trillion deficit in just the first nine months of the year and it will increase by $500 billion more by the end of the fiscal year. Finally, the national debt rose to 60 percent of gross domestic product–the largest US debt in history.

And prospects for the future? Perhaps that is best reflected by a *Wizard of ID* cartoon strip by Parker and Ross: The ruler of the kingdom of ID goes to a fortune teller. She peers into a crystal ball. "What do you see?" the monarch asks in earnest. The fortune teller waits for a heartbeat and then replies, "I see pain. I see misery. I see woe." The monarch's reply: "I know. I know. But what about the future?"

That frustration is evident across our nation.

The general consensus is that recovery will be a slow process. We wouldn't bet the ranch that it will happen by the 2012 presidential election, although the current administration will argue vehemently that, "It did." It may be a long time until we see the previously acceptable 5 percent unemployment again.

So with this macroeconomic quicksand all around us, let's turn our focus to American higher education.

A few years ago, while I was president of Stephen F. Austin State University in Texas, I drove the 200 miles from Nacogdoches to Austin on short notice. There were budget constraints that year. I sat with the presidents of the state universities and we reviewed the depressing situation. All our glasses were definitely less than half full that year.

Immediately after the focused and intense meeting, I hopped into my car and rushed back to campus. We called a campus-wide meeting, and a large number of faculty and staff attended. I meticulously went through the state's dire economic situation and reviewed what financial morsels might be coming forth for Texas public universities. When the meeting ended, I was feeling a bit better after sharing the bad news. Then, standing by a punch bowl, one of the faculty senate leaders leaned toward me and whispered, "Do you think any of that will affect *us*?" I was speechless! The answer then was "YES!" for that university just as the answer now is emphatically "YES!" for American higher education.

*US News & World Report* Editor Brian Kelley lays it on the line: "Of all the industries that profited from the economic bubble of the past two decades...higher education would have to be at the top of the list." He points to massive endowments, soaring tuition that regularly eclipsed the cost of living, extensive campus building, bloated administrative staffing, and says that some professors were being recruited like rock stars. He believes that "the golden age" has passed higher education by and that higher education should change.

We agree. But it is not a matter of *should, can* or *could* change; it is now a matter of *must change*. Higher education, like the automotive industry, has denied and ignored the call for reform for so long that it has painted itself into a corner. The growing forces gathering outside the campus walls for the past couple of decades are about to gain tsunami force and smash the venerable but vulnerable ivory tower into smithereens.

Let's tee-off on the world of golf where a massive shake up is taking place also. As Jon Swartz of *USA Today* notes, "The business of golf faces an economic outlook that is sinking like a downhill putt." Swartz says that about three in twenty of the more than 4,000 private golf clubs face dire financial circumstances and that the number of golfers is in a downward spiral.

There is a lesson for higher education in this.

Let's examine the major reasons for the fall-off in golf.

First, golf is expensive. You can drop $200 a day or considerably more to play on an elite course-without adding in the cost of clubs, shoes, balls and accessories which all are costly. In order to become a high-grade golfer, add in the cost of lessons from a golf pro-even more expensive. Second, it takes a substantial amount of time to play eighteen holes, not counting travel time to and from the course, and adjusting your schedule to fit with available tee times that seem never to be set at your convenience.

Doesn't golf sound a lot like a traditional college campus? Tuition, which is already high, continues to rise along with increasing book costs; classes are scheduled at the institution's convenience; students anticipate studying with a pro but often end up with a graduate-student instructor, while paying the same rate regardless. Worse, the odds are less than fifty-fifty that you will finish the "eighteen holes" with a degree in four years and not much better that you will have developed the level of skill you'd expected to achieve when you first arrived on campus.

Speaking plainly, the academic Model T has been so unresponsive to needed change that it might as well have painted a bull's eye on its institutional backside. In truth, the holes are greater than the sum of the parts and converging trends are kicking higher education's butt.

As a result one college student in ten today is enrolled in a for-profit, post-secondary educational institution. Tuition and fees over the past twenty five years have gone up by 400 percent (even before the 7 percent increase for FY 2010). That's four times the rate of inflation. (Did anyone actually believe that could go on forever?) University endowments have been particularly hard hit at the Ivy League schools where the average university endowment lost 18 percent in FY 2009.

The online revolution is no longer new, except in the higher education world. The rise of other nations in terms of economy, capability and aspirations hasn't been internalized; and like the GM Chevy Nova that didn't sell well in Latin America, leaders in higher education have demonstrated no *VA*! They cluster in "group think" waiting on federal and state government policy directives and private foundation money to fuel needed changes.

It's as if American higher education's hundred-year-old footprints are embedded in cement while the rest of the world is running at warp speed. Higher education has shrugged off the launch of numerous Sputniks when it desperately needs to respond to the challenges of the twenty-first century.

Pick your vantage point and adjustments are being made everywhere else. The domestic airline industry lost 69 million passengers over the past two years. Mounted police have dwindled to less than 100 in the nation. Pay telephones are nearly extinct and will be the next to go. (Have you hunted for one lately?) And hard lines will be the next thing to go.

Meanwhile military recruitment is up. In 2009, the Pentagon announced that for the first time since 1973 (when it became an all-volunteer force), the US military had met all its recruitment goals.

Casinos are returning to penny slots. Over the past two years in Nevada, casinos made way for 7,000 additional penny slot machines while removing almost twice that number for bigger bets.

College textbooks are going rental. With prices soaring four times the rate of inflation since 1994, Follett and Barnes & Noble (the two largest college bookstores in the nation) are making about 40 percent of their titles available for rent. They are also going electronic with Kindles and iPads.

Amazon's stock is soaring while Barnes & Noble is looking for a buyer.

Netflix has replaced Blockbuster and is in itself now being challenged by Apple and Amazon.

Lifestyles are changing. The number of commuters driving to work alone has dropped while the number of Americans owning only one car or no car has risen. The number of families living with three generations under one roof has increased.

Even cemeteries are responding. Although the industry may seem recession proof, 40 percent of cash-strapped families are turning to less expensive cremations where they can save more than half of the $7,000 average traditional burial cost.

But even as Americans shift their taste for cars, cruises, clothes and exotic vacations, there are some areas that have not shown signs of shrinkage: ice cream, movies and candy. In fact, Snickers and Three Musketeers were brought to market during the Great Depression. These treat items send a psychological message that says, "We're okay."

Deep down though Americans know we are *not* all right. We know that things have to change in a significant and profound way. It's paradigm time! One recent cartoon makes the point: In a crowded bat cave, the head bat is leading a meeting. After the issue has been discussed, he says, "All right, all in favor put your hands *down.*"

This book is not about curing the ills of the Great Recession. It is not about national or international economic policy. It is not about housing, banking or taxation. The issue here is American higher education, which is not immune to the mega-forces affecting our way of life. As the higher education reporter and pundit Jack Stripling observes, there is a gigantic gap between talk and action: "conversations have persisted for decades without substantial changes."

American higher education finds itself in a condition similar to Oakland, California's Bay Bridge. The bridge was considered an engineering wonder when completed in 1936. More than a decade ago a Caltrans study warned that the eastern span of the bridge could not withstand a 6.5 earthquake. Consequently, the bridge will not be retrofitted; it is schedule to be replaced. But not until 2013! Most everyone agrees that higher education requires restructuring, but few are responding to this crisis with any true sense of urgency, much to our detriment as a society.

This book explores the current condition of American higher education, making a case for bold and constructive change. The book was not written from inside the university looking out. Rather, the perspective is from the outside looking in by two university administrators who bring a wealth of off-campus and on-campus experience, multi-level business and governmental exposure, and who know their subject well.

We invite you to join us in this unusual and eyebrow-arching journey. But first take our Higher Education Awareness Test and feel the HEAT.

# HEAT
## Higher Education Awareness Test
## (Mark Your Answer True or False)

_____ 1. About 40 percent of Americans over age twenty-five have a college degree.

_____ 2. Most college students are under age twenty-two.

_____ 3. Online college courses typically cost less than in-person courses.

_____ 4. For-profit universities are allowed to receive up to 90 percent of their tuition revenue in the form of federal education loans and grants.

_____ 5. Endowments at private universities were largely insulated from the effects of The Great Recession by conservative investment policies.

_____ 6. Since the onset of the Great Recession, state colleges and universities have generally held tuition increases below the rate of inflation.

_____ 7. Despite the increase of for-profit and online universities, most US college students still attend school in the traditional four-year residential setting.

_____ 8. The average "discount rate" (the amount private colleges actually charge students) is 10 percent less than the sticker price.

_____ 9. The World Economic Forum's 2010 Global Competitiveness Report lists America as among the top in all twelve categories.

_____ 10. China uses more energy than the US.

continued . . .

_____11. In terms of college degrees, younger Americans (age twenty-five to thirty-four) have made significant gains in the past thirty years.

_____12. CalPERS, the largest public employee retirement system in the nation, once predicted that the Dow Jones Indus trial Average would be 25,000 by 2009.

_____13. "iGen" is a major breakthrough in computer technology.

_____14. Community colleges began by adding grades thirteen and fourteen to high school.

_____15. University presidents supported the start of community colleges.

_____16. Vice President Joe Biden's wife Jill is a community college instructor.

_____17. Most economists believe that state revenues will be back to normal by 2012.

_____18. Higher education spent more than $90 billion on new construction between 2002 and 2008.

_____19. Consumer **spending** drives 70 percent of our economy.

_____20. Traditional college students (ages eighteen to twenty-two) comprise 60 percent of today's college students.

_____21. Until 2010, California was the only state in the nation to require a two-thirds vote to pass both the state budget and a statewide tax increase.

_____22. Canada is the world leader in the higher education completion rate.

_____23. Forty-five of every 100 students who start college today will not earn a bachelor's degree.

_____24. It takes about six years for a student to finish a college degree.

_____25. The current outstanding student loan debt is larger than the entire TARP "bailout" or the whole Obama Stimulus Package.

*Answers found on page 219.*

# Part One: The View from the Dean's Office

Chapter I

# THE BIG SQUEEZE ON ALMA MATER

"Forget about business as usual.
There is no return to the way we were."
Greg Roberts, Executive Director
Association for the Promotion of Campus Activities

Although I am a business school dean, most of my professional career was spent as an investment banking executive. But before that I was a lawyer, so I tend to think in analogies. When I first started thinking seriously about the "business" aspects of a university, I tried to find the right analogy in the broader commercial world for what a university does.

We provide a "service" more than a "product." Higher education really is a "knowledge industry" in a classic sense, delivering its "content transfer" in a relatively discrete period of time with beginning and end points, usually at a "formative period" in the recipient's life, and focused on enhancing the recipient's future prospects.

After hours of mental gyrations, my first best analogy was orthodontics: the smile that opens doors for the rest of your life! Reflecting on the focus of this book, however, I knew that orthodontics just wouldn't do. Flying back to Palo Alto from a visit with family in New York, my brain turned quite naturally to air travel, and ultimately to the analogy I'd been seeking. And so that is where we begin our look at the "university business" one decade into the twenty-first century.

Of course, it would be good business school practice to start with a chapter about the university's "customer," the student. But to be fair to the facts, we need to start by looking at the university itself, because the current crisis in higher education is rooted in an institutional failure to focus primarily on its "customer" when the basic operating model was designed.

But for a moment, step back to the air travel analogy. Suppose you decided to take an around-the-world trip by air. With modern aircraft capabilities, you could make it in less than two days in three legs: say, San Francisco to Tokyo, then Tokyo to London and finally London to San Francisco. The airline, however, responds that you'll have to take at least four legs, maybe even five or six, because when you complete one leg, there might not be planes available for the next part of your journey. They also inform you that they won't be flying at all during the summer months. Ask why, and they will explain that the passengers are busy tilling fields and harvesting crops. Never mind that nobody actually does that anymore, the airline doesn't seem to notice or care. Their attitude is: "We've always done it this way and we're still around, so we must be right."

When it comes to cost, the airline says your ticket price is subject to upward adjustment at each leg. Of course you won't know what the increase for each leg is going to be in advance, but lately it's been as much as 32 percent!

Finally, you learn that you may get an experienced pilot on any particular segment, or you might have a trainee. And, by the way, you won't be able to use any of your Internet gear while on board. But you will be able to drink alcohol freely en route (although the passengers admitted to first class–the sons and daughters of previous passengers of that airline–will get served first).

Maybe only the last part of this fable sounds at all relevant to what's going on in US colleges and universities today. But if we look a little more closely a broader pattern of similarity emerges. Obviously you would not give your business to an airline with all these limitations on their service, or so you think. But what if all the available airlines operated on the same basis? Then you and all other would-be passengers would be stuck.

Sooner or later, however, you and the other passengers would understand that there is no reason why you can't get the service you want, especially given the price you are being asked to pay–and then, along comes an airline with the same planes flying to the same destinations, but offering a more customer-friendly approach to service.

The same thing is happening in the higher education marketplace today. Real competition has entered the picture, and in a big, new way. Of course, colleges have always competed among themselves for the best students, the most brilliant faculty and the most lucrative research grants. But we're talking here about a different kind of competition, the kind that happens when customers of any enterprise wake up to their power to shape the product they are buying. Up until recently, higher education considered itself relatively immune from this kind of customer-driven market force.

Like many other knowledge-based professions (medicine, law, investment banking) colleges traditionally have considered themselves exceptions to the rule that "The customer is always right". Colleges think it is *their* job, after all, to teach their customers exactly what *is* right. If their stock-in-trade is instruction, then students, like patients or clients, have no business telling them how to run their operation. Nice work if you can get it!

But like those served by medicine, law and high finance, students (and their parents and other "financiers") have begun to flex their bargaining muscles, especially as the cost of educational services rapidly accelerates beyond the ability to pay without real pain.

At some tipping point (say, double-digit tuition increases), the price of education reaches a level where the students (and their funders) come to understand that they are dealing with what should be–but isn't–one of the most customer-centric enterprises on the face of this earth. At the same tipping point, some higher educational providers also perceive that there is an advantage in paying much more attention to customer service.

In the heady time of dot-com and housing bubbles, this recognition of "students as customers" focused more on "frills" that could ease students past the sleepy essence of the academic service culture: i.e., the "bread and circuses" of campus life–luxurious, co-ed dormitories, state-of-the-art gyms and health centers, magnificent stadiums and fully professionalized sports programs funded by tax-deducting boosters, TV revenue, university subsidies and hefty student fees. But recessions make a hash of bread and circuses. More importantly, recessions expose rampant inefficiencies in the supply chains of even the most hidebound knowledge-based enterprises, especially a delivery system that works at capacity only about two-thirds of the "expense year."

The "Great Recession" has created a perfect storm for the US higher education culture. Just when student/customers began to understand that if they are paying the check they should be able to order the meal, along came a dramatic downturn in state tax revenue and private endowment investment income that brought to an abrupt end the game of buying off students with frills. On top of that, the exclusive "franchise" that state-funded and private nonprofit colleges and universities had enjoyed for decades was challenged, precisely on customer-service terms, by *for-profit* educational enterprises funded by equity markets that are ever alert to the opportunities presented while established academies slept on their laurels.

While the newer, Wall Street-funded for-profit colleges initially focused their powerful marketing attention on chronically underserved student populations (particularly working adults), they also aggressively reached out to a more upscale population by exploiting the Internet, which most public and private schools viewed (correctly) as a threat to their established service cultures. As Richard Vedder, director of the Center for College Affordability observed, "The for-profits are concentrating 100 percent of their effort on teaching students what they want to be taught, when they want to be taught."

Nonprofit and state-funded colleges have no shortage of smart people, and many are certainly aware that the ground is shifting under their caps and gowns. Charging their customers ever-rising prices for increasingly outdated service delivery models is no longer as easy a "sell" as it has been. A few schools have been able to use state government and endowment funds to open educational doors to underserved populations (in the middle class and below) and to adopt new Cyber-based learning technologies that bring higher education into the "24/7" reality where customers now expect to be served. But the Great Recession also put a fiscal spanner into these good works, forcing colleges to make difficult choices between what they need to do and what they can afford to do.

This is especially the case with budget-starved state institutions. Recession-struck taxpayers have had enough of subsidizing the education of college and graduate students regardless of their financial need, not to mention paying increasing salaries to tenured faculty who have guarantees against lay-offs that few other taxpayers enjoy. For example, in November 2010 the *Chronicle of Higher Education* reported that voters in Washington State had rejected ballot propositions that would have authorized a $100 million bond issue for education facilities and an income tax surcharge on individuals making over $200,000 per year earmarked for education services, among others. New Mexico voters similarly turned down a $155 million bond issue for capital improvements in state university facilities.

States long committed to excellence in higher education have radically reduced their direct education funding. In terms of their histories of using college degrees to promote economic development and social mobility, states are shifting from "Mission Accomplished" to "Mission Abandoned." Many elite nonprofit universities abandoned that mission long ago, and likewise now find it hard to reclaim it as their endowments suffer from wrong-headed financial bets.

The adverse effects of consumer-driven competition combined with the Great Recession have been shared to a considerable degree by public and private universities. But the variances in impact in terms of budgetary and other factors are worth examining separately.

**The Big Squeeze on Public Universities**

By the start of the first decade of the twenty-first century, the value of a college degree had become so well established in the public mind that taxpayers were beginning to question the commitment of a substantial portion of state budgets to subsidizing the cost of higher education for both rich and poor alike.

The disparity in lifetime income between those with a college degree and those without has been clear for decades. Beginning in the 1970s, however, the link between education and opportunity became both stronger and more transparent in economic and cultural terms. According to a 2006 census analysis in the *Chronicle of Higher Education*, the earnings differential in favor of those with college degrees over high school graduates had increased from 36 percent to 76 percent, amounting to $1 million over a working lifetime. The wage gap continued to grow even though the supply of college-educated workers increased. The gap between average yearly earnings of college graduates as compared with high school graduates had grown from $18,000 to $22,000 per year, and for those with graduate degrees the gap against high school grads had increased to

$45,000 a year.

Other significant advantages have consistently accrued to college graduates. In 2009 almost 95 percent of individuals with college degrees enjoyed employer-based healthcare coverage compared with 77 percent of high school graduates and 67 percent for high school drop-outs. Similarly, almost 90 percent had access to employer-provided pension plans compared with 81 percent for high school graduates and 53 percent for dropouts. In the wake of the Great Recession, those with college degrees were only half as likely to become unemployed as high school graduates.

Even before the recent economic collapse, the college advantage was becoming so clear that across the country state legislatures were increasingly reluctant to continue to fund even their flagship universities at the same levels as before. The message from taxpayers was loud and clear, pushing state institutions to emulate private colleges by increasing tuition well beyond the rate of inflation and by seeking outside (non-taxpayer) sources of revenue, including aggressive recruiting of "full tuition" students from out-of-state. By 2004 for example, 72 percent of tuition revenue at the University of Colorado was being generated by the 30 percent of students from outside the state.

As competition for lucrative out-of-state students intensified, public universities were slowly but surely drawn away from their historic mission of providing educational access to the sons and daughters of their own states' taxpayers whose modest means might not otherwise provide for a university education. The State of Virginia, for example, had by 2004 reduced its contributions to UVA's $1.7 billion operating budget to 8 percent from a level of 28 percent two decades earlier. Other states were following suit. A 2004 *BusinessWeek* article noted that, while no public university had yet been fully privatized, "creeping privatization" was accelerating a broader movement by the top 100 state flagship institutions to increase tuition by double-digit rates, squeezing out the poor. Four-year public colleges had raised tuition by 90 percent on aggregate in the preceding decade.

The overall result is that public universities that were designed to provide broader access to higher education were turning more into private enclaves open primarily to the sons and daughters of relatively wealthy families. At Ohio's Miami University, for example, the median family income had already topped $100,000 by 2004. In the same year, the entering freshman classes at the nation's 146 most selective colleges and state flagships, included just 3 percent from the bottom socio-economic quartile, while 74 percent came from the top quartile. Five years later, after the onset of the Great Recession, state universities were moving even more aggressively to cut the financial ties between the taxpayer and academia, while still pursuing the strategy of raising tuition beyond the rate of inflation and pursuing full-tuition-paying students from outside their borders.

In 2009 the American Association of State Colleges and Universities (AASCU) detailed just how adversely the Great Recession had affected state budgets across the country and their ability to continue funding higher education in the face of other priorities. The states, in aggregate, cut $102 billion to address shortfalls in FY 2009, having suffered the largest drop in tax collections in the last half century, and were agonizing over $120 billion in additional shortfall for FY 2010.

That same study also projected a dire outlook for long-term recovery. Revenues based on conservative projections were coming in far below anticipated amounts in most states. Personal income tax receipts, which comprise about a third of state funds on average, were down more than 25 percent. In some states, such as Arizona, that negative percentage was much higher. As the *Chronicle of Higher Education* concluded in the spring of 2010, "Even when the economy does begin to bounce back state revenues typically lag recovery by at least two years."

The impact of declining tax revenue on academic resources has been severe for public higher education across the country. In early 2010, Florida State University laid off twenty-one tenured and fifteen tenure-track faculty. In the prior year, the University of Florida had eliminated eighty-one faculty positions (2 percent of the total), and increased its student/faculty ratio to twenty-to-one, among the nation's highest. Also in 2009, 121 faculty and 123 staff positions were left vacant at the University of Georgia, where some employees were also forced to take six furlough days a year. While at the University of Wisconsin, employees were forced to take eight furlough days and state grants were cut for about 20,000 eligible low-income students.

In 2009, Rutgers University in New Jersey delayed faculty raises to avert hundreds of layoffs. The absence of funding from either state or private credit markets for capital improvements also forced Rutgers to move some entering students into hotels because the crunch of dormitory space could not be relieved without new construction. In 2010 the University of Nevada, Reno announced plans to close its College of Agriculture and other academic departments to meet an $11 million mandatory budget cut. In South Carolina, higher education spending in the state had dropped by 2009 to roughly 1995 levels. The State of Hawaii cut faculty salaries by 6.75 percent, effective January 1, 2010. Although the University of Michigan was able to avoid major cutbacks with tuition increasing private fundraising and general "belt-tightening," officials considered eliminating a "Promise Scholarship" that had been providing millions in scholarship dollars for needy Michigan residents. Late in 2010, North Carolina Governor Beverly Perdue warned that state's public universities that they should increasingly rely on private gifts and grants as revenue sources—including to help pay for research—in the face of continuing public budget shortfalls. Even the Texas University System, which had been sheltered from some of the worst impacts of the Great Recession by the state's oil-based economy, was forced to freeze hiring for many positions system-wide, and UT Austin began laying off staff members in 2009 to free up funds to recruit and retain top professors.

Of course, continuing state budget cuts mean that larger proportions of state universities' budgets must be funded by tuition and fees, making "full tuition" out-of-state students an attractive target. More state universities accordingly are aggressively pursuing such students. For example, the University of Massachusetts announced plans in 2009 to double out-of-state enrollments and a similar focus is occurring at the University of Wisconsin, which draws 35 percent of its students from beyond state borders.

Douglas S. Greenbird, executive dean at Rutgers University School of Arts and Sciences, noted that "the temptation for us to recruit more out-of-state students is very common and very strong." But each nonresident place means one less slot for a New Jersey resident, leaving Rutgers with only two options: get bigger or increase tuition. "Every time tuition goes up we increase the possibility that we become more like a private university," Greenbird concluded.

Moreover, "getting bigger" without attracting full-tuition payers from out of state only increases operating deficits, as schools suffer net losses on their in-state admits. The only other option for many state university systems is continued tuition increases for in-state students. Michigan aggressively pursued out-of-state students while raising in-state tuition 50 percent between 2004 and 2009. Such increases are likely to continue due to an overall state budget shortfall of $1.7 billion. Meanwhile the University of Colorado Regents, while proposing a 9 percent tuition jump for in-state students, held its rate for the out-of-staters it depends on to a 5 percent increase.

In several cases, annual in-state tuition increases have leapt to double digits. Nevada, Florida, Washington and Utah indicated their in-state tuition rates would grow in 2010-11 by 10 to 15 percent–an astronomically high multiple of projected consumer price inflation in the same period. And California, as is its nature, topped them all with a 32 percent increase over two years in its flagship UC system.

Meanwhile, cash-strapped families faced with "operating deficits" of their own have clearly been reconsidering the value proposition of *any* high-dollar educational investments, whether in-state or out-of-state, private or public. A September 2009 *Chronicle of Higher Education* report found that colleges that try to recruit more out-of-state enrollments have confronted "sticker-resistance" from middle-class families that might in the past have taken loans to cover tuition at a private university or a prestigious out-of-state public college.

Consumers of higher education are increasingly skeptical that colleges are doing all they can to keep costs in line and tuition affordable, as we will detail in Chapter II. In effect, state institutions are being hit by a "double whammy": just as they are finding it harder to attract high-tuition-paying out-of-state students, they are confronted with increasing demand from their own in-state residents for additional entry spots, which in turn would increase their operating deficits. As a result, many set in-state tuition as high as they can get away with, while reducing expenses by cutting course availability to the bone, which makes today's path to graduation a long hard slog.

Nowhere is this situation more acutely evident than in the State of California. Pay cuts of 5 percent for the president of the university system and other senior executives in 2009-10 were just a token response to the state's higher-education-budget dilemma. Coming into 2008-09, the California State University System lost 30 percent of its state general funds appropriations. Additional cuts imposed in the 2009-2010 fiscal year meant that the system had lost more than *two-thirds* of its baseline state support from the early 1990s. By mid-summer 2009, the UC Board of Regents had also approved a furlough plan requiring every employee to take between eleven and twenty-six days off during the school year without pay. Even the 32 percent two-year tuition increase added by the UC Regents will not be enough to make up for the budget shortfall and its dramatic negative impact on student access to the courses needed to graduate.

Taken together, the University of California, California State and California Community College systems were forced to turn away close to 300,000 students in the 2009-2010 academic year. At UCLA alone, 165 courses and 428 staff positions were cut, 162 hiring searches were cancelled and salaries were reduced by an aggregate $37 million, while applications were increasing at the rate of 9 percent, with half the applicants presenting high-school grade-point averages of 4.0 or better.

While lower cost options at local community colleges across the country have generally not been hurt quite as much by state funding cuts as four-year "flagship" institutions, California's deeply impacted community college system lost $520 million of its aggregate budget in fiscal 2009-2010, translating into more than 95,000 students losing their places. At Foothill-DeAnza College, one of the leading community colleges in California if not the nation, fully *one-third* of the student population was wait-listed for at least one class in the fall of 2009. At City College of San Francisco virtually the entire 2010 summer class schedule was cut to help close a $12 million budget gap.

At the same time, the California State University system announced that it would reduce its enrollment by 9 percent, or 40,000 students, forcing all twenty-three campuses to essentially close admission for the spring 2010 term. Both University of California and CSU top administrators say that each system needs about $1 billion more in annual funding to restore educational quality to a 2001 level–the last time those university systems were in relatively good fiscal health. But in California as elsewhere, pleas from university administrations to restore state funds have fallen on deaf ears.

While the California State University system received $716 million in one-time support from the federal stimulus package, that funding was only a temporary boost. (Across the country, the stimulus replaced $2.4 billion of the $2.8 billion of state college funding cut in 2009.) The CSU chancellor requested an additional $884 million in state support to supplement stimulus money and to meet an avalanche in applications for FY 2010-2011–up 53 percent over the prior year, as more California families turn to the cheaper options of "home-state" education. But there was virtually no chance that the chancellor's request would be honored by the state legislature.

In March 2010, the *Chronicle of Higher Education* headlined that state budget cuts were "pushing public colleges into peril" in California and in many other states. The consequence was that state support for higher education would be reduced to such low levels that the "new fiscal reality" could narrow institutional missions, reduce course offerings, and raise tuition. It came as no surprise then that the California State University Trustees approved another, two-step increase of 15.5 percent in fees to take effect in 2011.

State governments are being forced by their legislatures to begin a new dialogue regarding the specific roles of *each* element of multi-campus university systems and to tailor accountability measures focused on those discrete missions. Rather than continuing to focus on increasing tuition revenues and out-of-state enrollment growth, state legislatures are now looking to go forward with a "right-sizing" approach that provides low-cost options to low- and moderate-income residents, while at the same time ruthlessly weeding out duplication, inefficiency and procedures that add unnecessary cost.

The "default option" of getting into a fight over out-of-state enrollments with elite private institutions would likely be a fool's errand for many state universities, as well as a socially undesirable step away from their core missions. While state-supported colleges have been spared the problem of declining endowments common to private, nonprofit institutions, they have not been spared the necessity to revisit how their basic operating models and delivery systems address their missions. Stephen Portch, former chancellor of the University System of Georgia, advises that although "higher education is changing by virtue of 1,000 painful cuts," it won't be the same ballgame in the future. "This time," he warns, "it isn't coming back to normal."

Indeed, California may again be pointing the way forward to the "new normal." The president of the UC System, the state governor and the UC Board of Regents have announced their support for an initiative to create an "eleventh campus" for the system–one in which course offerings would be delivered entirely over the Internet. Although there is little funding immediately available for such an initiative, it introduces many possibilities about once again providing broad access, for *both* in-state and out-of-state students. For once, it appears, a state system has been forced to rethink itself for the sake of its "customer."

### The Big Squeeze on Private Universities

The too-easy money derived from financial "alternative investments" that triggered the Great Recession in the private sector also enticed the best-endowed private higher education institutions into ill-considered speculation in financial derivatives and private-equity bets. These proved almost as troublesome for them as they did for the "best and the brightest" on Wall Street.

The largest universities in the US faced over $38 billion in collective endowment losses for the fiscal year that ended June 30, 2009. Percentage losses at Harvard, Stanford, Princeton, Yale and the University of

Chicago each were in the neighborhood of 20-25 percent. Harvard, which has long held the richest endowment, had the largest one-year loss of nearly $11 billion. A study by the National Association of College and University Business Officers found that overall endowments at 842 institutions of higher learning experienced an average 18.9 percent decrease for that fiscal year.

The effects of the Wall Street portfolio model on investments at five major New England universities "wreaked havoc, jeopardizing the security of academic programs" according to a study by the Center for Social Philanthropy at Boston's Tellus Institute. The study cited fiscal 2009 losses of 17.5 percent at Boston College, 22.1 percent at Boston University, 21.6 percent at Brandeis, 22.8 percent at Dartmouth and 20.7 percent at MIT. The study suggested that the presence of many financial industry executives on university boards was creating at least the appearance of conflicts of interest, perhaps leading to reluctance to change investment practices. The results of these practices, however, while not out of line with the general effects on other private investments during the height of the Great Recession, did bring on some serious programmatic belt-tightening even at the most prestigious colleges.

In the wake of endowment losses, the Harvard University School of Arts and Sciences announced a retirement program for up to 127 professors, and included options for professors over age sixty-five to wind down their work over one, two or four years, resulting in an 18 percent decrease in the 720-member faculty. Stanford University cut 420 staff positions, including an equivalent of nearly 20 percent of its Development Office of 250 people. Stanford also asked each department for a 15 percent budget cut, cancelled or delayed $1.4 billion in proposed construction projects, instituted selected hiring freezes, and reduced the number of active faculty searches.

For some of America's most elite private universities, however, the impact of the Great Recession on their endowments will amount to a "speed bump" that will not seriously jeopardize their ability to provide high quality education for their "highly selective" cohorts of students. The repercussions felt by a broader range of private colleges and universities however are much more severe.

Many independent nonprofit schools followed the elite schools' pattern of investments in alternative assets, but lacked deep endowment cushions. The spending binges at many of these institutions reflected the mentality of the now infamous housing "bubble." Many gorged on cheap credit for construction, technology and creature comforts even as their relatively smaller endowments began to decline. As the cost of those new assets began to eat into their operating budgets, they struggled to extract higher tuition and fees from cash-strapped families who were dealing with their own problems from the effects of the Great Recession.

As a result, many private institutions will be forced to change what they do to survive. They may merge with bigger schools or even sell themselves to for-profit institutions to avoid closing down. Sandy Baum, a senior policy analyst for the College Board cited by *Bloomberg*, put it bluntly: "Small colleges with no reputation could well go out of business particularly the more they are tuition driven." Others estimated as many as 200 independent colleges lack the capital to meet their expenses in the long run, especially as the Great Recession's effects persist into the next decade.

Similarly, many private educational institutions must also adjust their own expectations downward in view of the new economic realities. As a report in *Barron's* in June 2009 summarized, the "Big Squeeze" has hammered the endowments of colleges that followed an investment portfolio policy designed to provide optimal returns with allegedly relatively low risk through a disproportionate allocation to hedge funds, private equity, real estate and commodities. The simple truth is that there will be no return to their "old normal" in the wake of the Great Recession.

Byron Wien, the respected former senior analyst at Morgan Stanley, was cited by *Barron's* as observing that the investment "portfolio model" used by elite universities is now dead. "The idea used to be that every asset had a predictable return and volatility based on history. *History, however, is less useful now*." (Emphasis supplied.) Wein's observation is an excellent summary of where private universities of a certain size and market presence find themselves today.

In addition to sharply declining endowment values, private colleges are facing a decline in private giving as well. Donations declined by almost 12 percent ($3.7 billion) in 2009. Private liberal arts colleges were the hardest hit, with an 18.8 percent decline. Alumni support fell to an average of 10 percent, the lowest level ever recorded, and the average gift from alumni declined 13.8 percent.

As a result, some prestigious private universities are being forced to "triage" their programs for the first time in ages. A Brandeis University committee, for example, recommended in early 2010 that twenty-four faculty members and a range of academic programs, such as theater design and anthropology, be eliminated due to shortfalls in endowment earnings and donations.

Some colleges are still tempted to bet on a return to the "old normal" in both the financial markets and the economy generally. But more likely they will be faced with adjusting to a "new normal" in their operating plans. The days of floodlit pools and student apartment complexes resembling luxury five-star hotels are trinkets of the past at most private universities.

Many undergraduate schools that had turned to borrowing in order to fund physical and technological amenities to entice students now find themselves drowning in debt that they cannot service. And new buildings and staffing increases intended to achieve specialized accreditations now constitute more of a burden than a benefit with the shift in "family values" toward less expensive state-funded institutions.

During the spending binge before the Great Recession, many schools continued to jack-up tuition at rates significantly above inflation, counting on the bull-market wealth of parents and rising endowment values to fund future operating budgets. When the credit markets collapsed in 2008, schools that had over-borrowed and over-spent faced a sudden, debilitating liquidity crisis. The same credit-rating agencies whose practices and judgments had facilitated the ability of these schools to borrow in easy-credit markets have put a post-recession squeeze on these schools to fundamentally change their business models in order to survive. For example, in April 2009, Moody's determined that increasing credit risks had changed its general outlook for the higher education sector to "negative" from "stable." The number of downgrades to college credit ratings in the first three quarters for 2009 was almost twice that of all 2008, and the number of "negative outlooks" published during that year out-paced the number for all of 2008 by 50 percent. Nearly all rated colleges and universities reported weakened balance sheets for the 2009 year.

Smaller private institutions will not have the luxury of time or circumstance to bring their bloated balance sheets back to health. The rating agencies have laid down clear markers for assessing the ability of universities to survive in this new environment. Moody's called special attention to A- and BAA-rated private colleges, which are far less diversified in their revenue sources than AAA- and AA-rated schools, and are more dependent on tuition revenue. Moody's noted that while the multi-billion-dollar federal stimulus program was adding funds to help the public sector and research universities in significant ways, a much smaller proportion of such stimulus dollars was passed on to private colleges and universities.

Moody's identified fourteen specific warning signs that could trigger further rating reviews and downgrades for higher education institutions, including: rising operating deficits; qualified audit opinions; unexpected increases in debt; defaults under bond covenants; and exposure to a high proportion of debt at variable rates of interest. Universities that had invested in derivatives and swaps experienced significant declines in the fair value of those investments and Moody's observed those universities would be forced to post large amounts of cash collateral with their counterparties (the same problems AIG got itself into in its end game).

In pointing the way forward to mitigate these serious financial stresses, Moody's identified steps that private universities could take to slow their capital and operating spending and build liquidity. Moody's especially called for improved disclosure as well as changes in management practices at the top level of universities, including the development of multi-year financial plans.

As Moody's predicted as early as October 2008, private schools, like state universities, also face emerging resistance to ever-increasing tuition and fees. That prediction has come true as more and more students and their families have adjusted their sights downward in terms of the "cost-value" continuum.

As private colleges in financial distress are forced to rethink their business models, the great temptation will be to mirror the out-of-state tuition hunt underway at public universities by increasing tuition *discounting* in order to sustain or increase enrollment. According to the *Chronicle of Higher Education*, freshman discount rates at four-year schools had increased to an average of nearly 40 percent even in pre-recession 2007 (up from 37 percent a decade earlier). More recently, *InsideHigherEd.com* reported that in 2009 the discount rate for entering freshman had increased to 42 percent, well above the 35 percent level that experts consider to be the trigger for financial risk. (Colleges should bear in mind that such desperate discounting practices could not at the end of the day save the American automobile industry.) Nonetheless, the price of enrollment shortfalls without serious tuition discounting will be severe. Some private nonprofit schools have been forced to suspend retirement contributions for employees, impose furloughs and eliminate administrative and support positions for programs that attract the smallest enrollments. Such traditional "muddling-through" measures were employed after previous recessions, but those did not have the same severity as the 2007-2010 financial meltdown.

For most colleges, managing in this new era has meant a period of "hunkering down," as the *Chronicle of Higher Education* pointed out in late 2009. But the coming months and years could require far more openness to structural change. As one university official observed, "It's not a paradigm shift; it's an adjustment to the cost structure in response to a large shock." This kind of understated euphemism has become common in these post-recession times! A more blunt assessment of the situation came from Dick Niemiec, interim president of Beloit University, as he prepared his 2009-2010 budgets on the assumption that his university would suffer a modest enrollment shortfall: "If the economy doesn't bounce back within a year, then, like other businesses, *we'll have to change our model*." (Emphasis supplied.)

Turning on a dime (especially if it's a borrowed dime) is not the easiest thing to do in the tradition-bound private university culture. But the more astute managers of private institutions have recognized that the landscape has changed. As David Wheaton, vice president for finance and administration at Minnesota's Macalester College observed, "We stepped through the looking-glass and now things are different." Macalester undertook serious efforts at multi-year planning for an uncertain future, examining a range of variables that reveal what the university would look like under varying financial conditions. This kind of openness to change is the "looking glass" into the "new normal" that faces private higher education in the US.

To summarize the situation for both public and private nonprofit colleges and universities as we begin to emerge from the Great Recession, we see a tangle of cross-currents forcing all but the most elite to seriously rethink their operating structures.

State institutions must face increasing demand for lower-priced educational options from in-state families who are financially struggling from the recession. At the same time, the colleges and universities are experiencing severe reductions in taxpayer-provided resources and increasing reluctance of out-of-state families to fund full-priced tuition.

Private institutions not of medallion status confront declines in contributions from their donors, shrunken endowments and a reduced ability to "borrow their way through," as well as the same reluctance by families to go into debt to fund high-priced tuition, not unlike their state university counterparts. Collectively these circumstances will pressurize the inefficiencies and frills in both types of universities' formerly stable business models. Educational "business as usual" is no longer an option.

Change—indeed, *disruptive* change—is coming to higher education. And that change will be driven by two fundamental facts: it has never been more important to America that Americans have access to a college education; but it has never been more difficult to afford it. For both public and private schools, the central question is how the consumers of education (students and their families) will be able to fund their own investments in higher learning.

Lee Higdon, then-president of the public College of Charleston and later president of the private Connecticut College, argued presciently in a 2003 article in *University Business* that budget crises should force universities to focus intensively on their specific missions and recalibrate their programs to fit the mission, which sometimes means moving away from what he called the "academic supermarket" mentality of the 1990s. Many public and private universities failed to heed that advice and indeed moved back into the supermarket model just before the financial crisis of 2007-10. President Higdon's words of warning in 2003 were right on the mark: "Getting through will require creative structure and nontraditional thinking; but aren't those the very skills we want to instill so that our children continue to prosper?"

More recently, Charles Miller, who served as chair of the Administrative Commission on the Future of Higher Education under President George W. Bush, concluded that most universities had not made fundamental changes but continued to react in typical fashion to financial stress by looking for new government funding and by cutting staff and programs. The alternative, according to Miller, is to find new ways to be more productive with existing resources. As we shall see in Chapter II, this is precisely what American college consumers are now expecting colleges to do.

From a business school dean's perspective, it would not be a bad idea at all to start this rethinking from the point of view of the student/customer, rather than from the traditions of the present day university structure.

Chapter II

# GRADUATION GRIDLOCK

"We are heading for a precipice."
Bill Conley
Johns Hopkins University

Forty years ago (back in my NYU days), the question set to music was "Where have you gone, Joe DiMaggio?" Today's question in the US university community might be "Where have you gone, Joe College?" The answer: gone to work; gone deeply into debt; and all too often, *not* gone on to graduate. In the future, the answer will often be: "gone online."

According to the US Department of Education, only about 40 percent of those who begin their higher education at four-year institutions graduate within six years, and only about 20 percent of students at community colleges earn an associate's degree within three years. While nearly 90 percent of high school seniors say they want to go to college, nearly 50 percent of those who actually start college eventually drop out. While a much higher proportion of high school graduates are in college today than a quarter century ago, that increase has not been met by a commensurate increase in the population of those who actually earn a degree, according to the National Bureau of Economic Research. In short, American higher education is beset by "graduation gridlock." Indeed, the likely percentage of college graduates among those who entered in 2009 will be lower than any time since the 1970's–45 percent are projected to drop out before finishing a bachelor's degree. The NBER Report also found that the decrease in the college-completion rate is worst among students attending public colleges and universities.

Public institutions face a harsh trade-off between providing access by keeping tuition low and raising tuition (which in turn reduces access) to provide resources to facilitate and support degree completion. A recent report prepared by Public Agenda (with support from the Bill and Melinda Gates Foundation) demolished the "Joe College" myth, and also exposed why so many students fail to finish college: they have to work to afford to attend, but can't square their work schedules with their class schedules.

While many Americans still think of college in terms of going to school full-time, living in a dorm, and enjoying extra-curricular activities, that is far from today's reality. According to the Public Agenda report, just "25 percent of students attend the residential college we often envision," and of that 25 percent who do attend in the traditional fashion, almost half work twenty hours per week. At community colleges, 60 percent of the students work at least twenty hours a week, and more than one-quarter work nearly full-time (thirty-five hours a week).

The number one reason students gave the researchers for the Public Agenda report for leaving school was *the pressure of having to work and go to school at the same time*. Balancing work and school was an even bigger barrier sometimes than finding money for tuition, although the rising cost of tuition is the major reason why students have to work during the school year in the first place! Additionally, drop-outs are left with the worst of both worlds: no diploma, and a large student-loan debt meant to be paid for with earnings from the job that a diploma could have brought.

Public perception of college students simply has not kept pace with today's reality. Fully 85 percent of all higher education students in the US are now "nontraditional" in one sense or another: age, work/life status, or other demographic measures. The Public Agenda study concluded that

American higher education faces a moral challenge in terms of helping the growing numbers of "nontraditional" students complete their education and enter the market economy.

Longstanding operating norms of American colleges and universities present serious issues for students who need to work and go to school at the same time–not the least being the traditional "academic calendar" of semesters or quarters covering nine months of the year with summers pretty much off, and with virtually all classes scheduled during week days only. Ironically, this academic calendar was originally designed to fit an agrarian work/life cycle, but now is a major impediment to those who have to fit school into work/life "clocks" that run "24/7."

The obstacles to graduation confronting today's students, of course, also include the overall high cost of tuition and fees. Among the nation's elite schools, fifty-eight private colleges charge at least $50,000 for the entire package of tuition, fees, room and board. The all-in price of college has grown at a much faster rate than the prices of other goods and services, according to The College Board. Between 1990 and 2008, tuition and fees rose a whopping 248 percent between 1990 and 2008–during that same period cumulative inflation nationwide was just under 66 percent! The average cost of tuition and fees has increased more than four times the rate of inflation, and twice the rate of medical costs, according to the National Center for Public Policy and Higher Education. As Bill Conley, dean of enrollment and academic services at Johns Hopkins University (where the total package amounted to $51,690 for the 2009-2010 academic year), told the *Chronicle of Higher Education*, "We are heading for a precipice" in terms of college costs.

If we did not have a "healthcare crisis" in this country, we would no doubt be focusing on an "education crisis" for the American middle class, which even before the Great Recession financed the ever-increasing costs for education by taking out massive loans (many tied to home-equity lines of credit). As long as college degrees seemed to secure a solid economic future for their children, parents were prepared to take the risks of indebtedness (especially with low borrowing costs). A May 4, 2009, article in *Bloomberg* observed: "One thing that has kept families paying these higher prices for higher education. . .[is] the return they expect their children to receive on the investment." *Bloomberg* also noted that it takes about ten years to recoup a $200,000 investment in a four-year college degree costing $50,000 per year.

Some critics among even liberal commentators have begun to question the relative value of a college degree. This skepticism has focused especially on whether public subsidies for colleges, direct or indirect, are justified vis-à-vis other possible ways of providing social and economic mobility for the disadvantaged. Economist Paul Krugman, for one, has expressed concern whether the public investment in state-sponsored universities is producing sufficient social returns.

John Shore, a tax expert at the Center on Budget Policy Priorities, in September 2009 put his finger on a basic change in the public mood: whereas in the past the state subsidized college access because it was deemed in the best interest of society, the balance of public opinion has shifted in favor of a system where students pay more and taxpayers pay less.

The continuing demise of blue-collar jobs with middle-class wages for workers with modest skills, however, suggests that college is not just a preferred path to economically rewarding careers, but increasingly it is the *only* road. Meanwhile the pipeline that moves students from admission to graduation is broken for both colleges and students alike. As *US News & World Report* put it, "Now that the economy has weakened, universities and undergraduates have been left grasping for ways to fill [their] budget gaps in the most difficult financial climate in decades."

Many age groups are poorer after the Great Recession than they were even in the recession-damaged 1970s. Household income for those in their peak earning years (between forty-five and fifty-four) slumped $7,000 between 2000 and 2008 after adjusting for inflation. This is the segment of the baby boom generation most impacted by core expenses for housing and cars as well as children, including the cost of higher education. To make up for their own cash-flow deficiencies when it comes to funding college, these households have been forced to borrow. College has become a "debt of necessity" not a "debt of choice."

Outstanding student-loan debt in the US now exceeds $800 billion–more than the TARP Wall Street bailout or the entire Obama stimulus package of 2009-2010. These borrowings have reached a point where a commentator in the October 12, 2009, issue of *The Atlantic Magazine.com* referred to the crunch of college-related debt as the "new form of indentured servitude."

The only escape from crushing burdens of college debt for financially stressed families has been the lower priced state universities. But just when public colleges are being swamped by applicants, they are being forced to raise tuition, and at the same time reduce enrollments, shut classroom doors, cancel courses, reduce extra-curricular programs, and cut back on faculty and staff. And these cutbacks, of course, exacerbate the "graduation gridlock" that shortchanges those students who have borrowed their way through school. As a result, low-income students who could benefit most from college are either being priced-out or hobbled with educational debt (whether or not they even graduate).Consumers who now wonder whether a house is worth $1,000 a square foot are also questioning (like Paul Krugman, but for different reasons) whether it is worth spending $1,000 a week to send their kids to college, especially if they have to mortgage their future to do so, according to a May 2009 commentary in the *Chronicle of Higher Education*.

The average American with a credit file carries more than $16,000 in debt, excluding mortgages. In this environment, borrowing for college is becoming an unprecedented burden on family finances. Unlike most debt (like residential mortgages) student loans are not dischargeable under bankruptcy, and thus do not enjoy "protection" like other forms of consumer credit. Failure to repay means that wages and tax refunds are subject to government seizure; credit ratings can be ruined; and borrowers in default can be denied rental apartments, mortgages, car loans and credit cards. Yet we now ask seventeen- to twenty-one-year-olds to try to assess how much student-loan debt they can handle vis-à-vis their incomes over their entire lives. And student futures are so much more uncertain now in the wake of the Great Recession.

A "Beyond the Crisis" *Financial Times* series underscored the new financial uncertainty for graduates in 2009: "That class graduated with unemployment for twenty- to twenty-four-year-olds in the US reaching a peak of 15.6 percent." Considering the aggregate number of these children of baby boomers, experts are worried about "a disproportionate effect on the economy as they move through life." Some cited by the *Financial Times* believe that the financial crisis will permanently damage the prospects for Generation Y. "Another 'lost generation' could be in the making, and long-term for the US economy that's terrible," according to Ellen Zentner, senior US macroeconomist at the Bank of Tokyo-Mitsubishi UFJ.

There is a growing sense among the public that higher education may be over-priced and under-delivered. A Public Agenda report in early 2010 focused on what it termed the "Squeeze Play"–continued public anxiety regarding college costs and increasingly harsher judgments on how colleges operate. The report tracked a series of national surveys on public attitudes towards higher education conducted by Public Agenda for the National Center for Public Policy and Higher Education. These surveys found Americans are far more skeptical about whether universities are doing all they can to control costs and keep tuition affordable. The report speculated that higher education may in fact have become a "soft target" in the public mind "where the price to consumer can be safely cut without either endangering the quality of education or curtailing the number of students who benefit." Of survey respondents, 54 percent agreed with the view that colleges could spend less and still maintain a high quality of education.

Public skepticism about college management developed in the wake of two important lines of thought that the Public Agenda surveys have tracked over the last two decades: a conviction that higher education is necessary for success in contemporary America, and an even stronger conviction that college is becoming less available to many qualified individuals. Those who think college is "absolutely necessary" jumped from 31 percent in 2001 to 55 percent in 2009. At the same time, however, seven in ten also believe that many qualified people can't get access to higher education. Importantly, most Americans surveyed believe that students are being forced to borrow too much to pay for college. This conviction has been hardened by their experience with a key effect of the Great Recession: namely, a big shift in views about debt in general and the prospects for paying it back. Although the survey results do not support a conclusion that the American public is turning its back on the value of higher education, the surveys do indicate that the public is rejecting the argument routinely made by university administrators that their institutions need ever more resources to fulfill their missions.

College presidents, of course, also feel squeezed between the costs of running their institutions and the number of students for whom they can provide a quality education. As a result, they argue that if they are to increase the number of students accepted *and* the quality of learning provided, they need more money; and continued budget cuts would mean fewer students graduating and lower-quality education. More "graduation gridlock."

But the majority of the public simply no longer buy that argument, according to the Public Agenda surveys. Most Americans surveyed believe that colleges could spend less and still maintain quality, and that higher education is mostly concerned about its own bottom line rather than the best education interests of its students. The survey concluded: "We find no evidence of sympathy for the argument that colleges and universities are starved for financial resources. . .the public may be in a period of ambivalence and unpredictability toward the financial difficulties of higher education." This brings us back to the "precipice" envisioned by the Johns Hopkins dean.

Is it also a "tipping point"? Longstanding academic operating policies seem profoundly ill-suited to students who simply cannot afford to borrow more to go to school and who have to work while they pursue their studies, or not pursue them at all. This situation powerfully demonstrates a need for flexible, *innovative* responses by colleges and universities–initiatives that will help Americans continue their education but in better-organized, more cost-effective ways.

The Gates Foundation study, cited at the beginning of this Chapter, pointed to a need for a "fresh, clear-eyed" look at current assumptions and practices in the university community. The study found that eight in ten of those who did not complete college supported two proposals they believed would make college graduation more feasible: making *part-time* students eligible for financial aid and offering more courses on evenings and weekends. While the levels of tuition and fees are highly important considerations for anyone in college today, among those who have dropped out the main issue is clearly the *inconvenience* of attending school while working.

It is precisely on the issue of convenience where for-profit institutions have stepped in with a zeal that could be setting the stage for the "new normal" of college life. Perhaps for-profit institutions, given their commercial nature, feel closer to economic realities (and opportunities) in terms of workforce-development needs, especially given the fact that by 2018 about 34 million workers will retire or shift occupations, requiring employers to scramble for their replacements. This represents more than two-thirds of more than 50 million job openings that are anticipated during that period–a greater rate of workforce replacements than employers have had to deal with in recent memory.

Currently more than 60 percent of businesses already face difficulty finding qualified skilled workers even with the loss of more than 8 million jobs since the Great Recession's onset. A professionally skilled workforce is key to the United States remaining competitive in global markets, and there is reason to worry that the US is no longer ahead of the pack in producing graduates with work-ready skills.

"Graduation gridlock" thus hurts business and the economy, too–not just Joe and Jane College. The jobs of the future are far more likely to require higher education than in the past. Already 31 percent of all jobs require some post-secondary education from vocational training to the PhD and within the next decade it will be 40 percent. Meanwhile the percentage of the population that completes college continues to lag behind.

The for-profit colleges purport to be highly focused on degree completion. In 2009 the number of degrees awarded during the previous decade by private for-profit institutions rose at a faster rate than the number conferred by public and private nonprofit colleges and universities, according to the *Chronicle of Higher Education*. This despite the fact that only about 8 percent of students attend for-profit institutions of higher education. More recent data from the National Center for Educational Statistics show that 60 percent of students seeking a two-year degree at for-profit colleges ultimately persist to graduation, compared with only 20 percent of students at public community colleges, despite the fact that the average tuition at public two-year community colleges is only about $2,500 a year, compared with $14,000 at for-profit institutions.

The most recent data available, however, show that many large for-profit universities have an abysmal record in terms of their students' attainment of four-year degrees, at least in terms of first-time, full-time students. A November 2010 report by The Education Trust ("Subprime Opportunity") found that in 2008, only 22 percent of students at for-profit colleges graduated within six years, compared with 55 percent at public institutions and 65 percent at private nonprofit schools. Only 9 percent of their first time, full-time students earn their bachelor's degrees in six years, and just 5 percent of the online students do so.

Meanwhile, tuition income at the for-profit colleges was funded by $4.3 billion in Pell Grants and $20 billion in federal loans in fiscal 2008-09, amounting to an average of 66 percent of their total revenue, with many close to bumping against the 90 percent overall limit (discussed in detail in Chapter IV). On the face of these attainment statistics, these federal expenditures appear to be an inordinately risky waste of taxpayer money, compounded by exposure to loan default risk. In a separate study, the Pew Research Center found that nearly 25 percent of those who earned bachelor's degrees at for-profit colleges borrowed more than $40,000, while only 5 percent of public-university students and 14 percent of private nonprofit college students needed that much borrowing to graduate. Not surprisingly, students graduating with degrees from for-profit institutions are typically much further in debt than their counterparts at public and private nonprofit schools–the median debt for bachelor's degree recipients at for-profit colleges is $31,190 compared with $17,040 at private nonprofits and $7,960 at public universities, according to the Education Trust. There is no easy escape from the grim cost-spiral that squeezes aspirations for a university diploma.

It seems worth considering whether community colleges might be the best prepared among public institutions of higher learning to rise to the challenge posed by the for-profit sector, especially among today's bargain-hunting college consumers. Indeed, the *Chronicle of Higher Education* concluded in a study forecasting the "college of 2020" that the strategic models of for-profit colleges and community colleges are likely to converge in the future. Each caters to older students who want and need courses that are available at flexible times and provided online that fit work/life schedules, more than they seek the traditional college experience.

The "new normal" for college education in the age of the working student may well take shape and form on the Internet. Indeed, the shift to online is already happening, as discussed in the next Chapter.

Chapter III
# ONLINE GAINS TRACTION

"Nothing is as likely to change the face
of higher education over the next decade
as the switch to online learning."
Chronicle Research Service

The public and nonprofit sectors of higher education heretofore have largely disdained, or at least ignored, the potential of Internet learning, as well as the working-adult-student market that online delivery serves very well. As for-profit institutions leapt headlong into both vacuums, the prevailing antagonism within traditional academic circles toward the for-profit model served to reinforce their resistance to online delivery.

Henry Levin, professor of economics at Columbia University's Teachers College, shared his disdain for the for-profit sector and online learning in spring 2010, saying that the model was based on "cheap labor" and providing what he termed a fixed curriculum. "Does it provide a degree equal to a middle-range business school? I don't think it does."

"I call it MBA-lite." John Fernandez, president and CEO of the Association to Advance Collegiate Schools of Business (AACSB), the primary special accrediting body for business schools and accounting programs, believes there is a "big quality differential between traditional and for-profit MBA programs." He advises students to "look at the other graduates and see how they're doing professionally." He also asks students to compare faculty credentials and see which other schools accept credits from for-profit institutions.

These cautionary and outright negative views buttress the long-time resistance in traditional academic circles to online learning formats precisely because online learning at the college level has long been identified primarily with for-profit schools. In retrospect, it is hard to understand how the smartest people in traditional education missed the signs that online learning had a future, but that resistance seems to be because they were not focused on serving nontraditional students.

Consider a May 29, 2009 commentary in the *Chronicle of Higher Education* in which opponents of online instruction contend that traditional face-to-face teaching is always superior and likened "giving in" to students' demand for online learning to giving in to their wish for free beer! Although some Internet-learning opponents may grudgingly accept the presence of some online courses as justified on the basis of factors like competition from other institutions in this struggling economy, they are nonetheless inclined to see online teaching as a second-best alternative—something to be tolerated, at best.

Of 183 nonprofit universities surveyed in a 2010 "Managing Online Education" study by the Campus Computing Project, nearly 75 percent cited resistance by their own faculties as a barrier to expanding online learning programs—more than all other impediments except budget cuts and lack of related support resources. And yet technology has fundamentally changed so many aspects of our information life (the way we get news reports, make purchases and communicate with others, especially through social media) that it is difficult to understand continuing resistance to applying online technology to education, the most fundamental "information industry" that mankind has ever known.

Online enrollments continue to grow much faster than overall higher education enrollment: up by nearly 20 percent from 2002 to 2007, compared with just a 1.5 percent increase in the overall college student population, according to a 2008 report from the Sloan Foundation. The study also revealed that more than 20 percent of American college students were already taking at least one online class in the fall 2007 semester–doubling the rates in just five years. By the fall '08 term online enrollment represented more than one-quarter of all higher education matriculation. Still academic officers in the broader higher education market continued to resist virtual learning. When asked whether their faculty would accept "the value and legitimacy" of online education a 2009 Sloan Foundation study found only three in ten chief academic officers said that their faculty members respect Cyber learning. The overall number who believe their faculty endorse online learning would have been even lower were it not for participation in the survey by community colleges and for-profit higher education institutions. A further Sloan report revealed that nearly 1 million more students took an online college course in fall 2009 than in the previous year–the biggest increase ever.

It should be no surprise that online higher education has continued to grow given the engagement of technology in the day-to-day life of adult learners, who represent the single fastest growing college population, a percentage that has been consistently increasing for the last three decades. Today only about 15 percent of college students fit the traditional model of eighteen- to twenty-two-year-olds attending full-time and living on or near campus. The nontraditional student population banks and pays bills online, shares digital photos and videos, purchases merchandise and services, downloads music and films, engages in social networks, reads and writes blogs and tweets, plots their travel routes to restaurants they've found online, and searches out new friends and relationships.

The vast majority of these adults are willing to consider online courses and degree programs, while a growing minority even reports a strong preference for online courses or at least a "hybrid" in-person/online program, according to recent surveys. Online programs deliver the kind of *flexibility* of class and study schedules that nontraditional adult students rank as among the most important considerations for both undergraduate and graduate programs. Older adults are even more likely to consider an online program than their slightly younger counterparts, according to a STAMATS 2008 survey ("Adult Students Talk Study™"). Among older adults (ages thirty-five to fifty-four) 71 percent said they would consider online programs compared with 60 percent of adults ages twenty-five to thirty-five. And increasingly, it's not just the students who value online education.

Online university degrees continue to gain popularity, legitimacy and prestige among corporate employers, according to an October 2010 *Reuters* article which cited a July 2009 survey of human resource professionals across industries. More than three-quarters of the respondents viewed online university degrees more favorably than they had just five years earlier. A majority of the respondents also believe that individual courses taken through online universities are as credible as traditional university courses. Fully 95 percent of respondents said there is no longer a difference in providing tuition assistance for employees studying at accredited online universities and those taking classes in traditional settings. A *Vault.com* study similarly reported that 83 percent of employers and hiring managers consider online degrees more acceptable than they had five years previously.

A 2009 US Department of Education evaluation of practices in online learning concluded that students who took all or part of their class work online performed *better* on average than those taking the same course through traditional face-to-face instruction. An earlier study cited by the *Chronicle of Higher Education* in November 2008 reported that online courses seem to stimulate more intellectual exchange and educational gains based on instructors' special efforts to engage students. Online students are just as likely as their campus-based peers to spend at least ten hours a week preparing for class and to participate in discussions, and to believe that their online campus environment is supportive of their academic success. As many observers have noted, in an online classroom there is no "back row" where students can hide out to avoid being called on or to sit out in-class discussions that can be shared and "threaded" transparently on the Internet among all the students in the class.

The steady resistance to online programs among traditional institutions of higher education provided the for-profit sector a golden opportunity to capture a significant "first-mover advantage."

A second fundamental reason for the success of for-profit online learning is directly traceable to federal "deregulatory" actions that removed substantial barriers to the expansion of for-profit institutions via the Internet. For-profit schools emerged from the shadows of trade and vocational education when they were able to obtain regional and national accreditation beginning in the late 1970s and into the 1980s, making their students eligible for federal education assistance programs. Expansion of for-profits during that period, however, was accompanied by numerous allegations of fraud and the re-emergence of the type of diploma-mills that had flourished earlier in the twentieth century.

In 1992 Congress enacted legislation to counter the rash of diploma-mill fraud, especially through so-called "correspondence" programs. The new law precluded any college that enrolled more than 50 percent of its students at a "distance" or which provided more than half of its courses via distance education from participating in federal student aid programs. (This, of course was pre-World Wide Web and few colleges, either traditional or for-profit, offered online courses.)

That 1992 legislation, however, authorized an eight-year experiment under which selected colleges received waivers of the 50 percent rule in order to test the efficacy of new forms of distance learning. Under this program, a few for-profit and nonprofit institutions such as Capella University and Texas Tech University ultimately were allowed to exceed 50 percent online enrollment for the experiment. Some participating institutions saw significant growth in their online enrollment.

A good example is Western Governors University, an all-online institution founded by the state governments of nineteen Western states, which experienced a surge in admissions topping 10,000 by 2007–a growth rate of 40 percent in each of the prior two years. While Governors is itself a nonprofit institution, the initial success of its "waiver" experiment, coupled with the election of a business-friendly national administration in 2000, spurred a serious lobbying campaign by the for-profit sector to liberalize the 50 percent rule to make more room for online degree offerings.

The Department of Education acted in 2002 first to secure elimination of the so-called "twelve-hour rule." In order for students to be eligible for federal financial aid, the rule required institutions that did not operate in a standard semester, trimester or quarter system to offer a minimum of twelve hours of coursework per week. For-profit educators had strongly advocated eliminating that rule, which they argued was inhibiting instructors from being innovative in online education programs. With support from the Bush Administration, Congress agreed to remove the rule effective in 2006 as part of the Deficit Reduction Act of 2005, and then also eliminated the "50 percent rule" on distance education offered through telecommunications such as the Internet or satellite broadcasting (leaving it in place only for the old-fashioned "correspondence" programs).

Although the 50 percent limit was eliminated, a requirement for accreditation "by an organization that was competent to evaluate distance-education programs" was continued in force. Such competence, however, was well within the purview of existing regional and national accreditors typically utilized by the for-profit sector. A further critical piece of the deregulation agenda under the Bush Administration occurred when the previous 75 percent limit on the amount of tuition funding that a school can receive from federal resources was increased to the current limit of 90 percent. This change has had tremendous impact on the US taxpayers' subsidy of higher education (for-profit style), as we shall see in Chapter IV.

With these significant deregulatory actions, the conditions for a rapid expansion of online higher education were fully in place. It is thus no surprise that along with the University of Phoenix and other much-larger institutions new for-profit schools like Bridgepoint, founded in 2005, and Grand Canyon University, taken over by online market entrepreneur Michael Clifford at about the same time have grown exponentially in enrollment and profits since deregulation. Even small new online universities like California Intercontinental University, based in Los Angeles, have been able to double in size within only a year.

Another major driver of online growth has been the exemption of military educational assistance programs from the 90 percent limit on federal tuition sourcing. According to *Bloomberg*, US taxpayers advanced $474 million for college tuition for 400,000 active duty personnel in the fiscal year ending in 2008–more than triple the spending for military tuition assistance a decade earlier. The lion's share of that assistance has fed into the expansion of for-profit online programs.

By expanding its military business, the University of Phoenix has been able to enroll more civilian students who are supported by grants and loans from the Education Department without violating the federal law limiting to 90 percent the revenue the school can receive from the government. A January 11, 2010, article in *Bloomberg/BusinessWeek* explained how the University of Phoenix derived 86 percent of its $3.77 billion of fiscal year 2009 revenue from the DOE, up from 48 percent in 2001. According to Gregory W. Capelli, co-chief executive of Phoenix's parent

Apollo Corporation, the university plans to stay below the 90 percent threshold precisely by building its military business, which counts in the denominator but not the numerator of the federal 90 percent ratio calculation.

American Military University, owned by American Public Education Corporation, counts more than 36,000 active duty students, up from only 600 in the year 2000. While some courses are held on base and some nonprofit colleges also participate in on-base learning programs, the highest active-duty college-course enrollment continues to belong to the online for-profit sector. Several for-profit online providers have adopted very "military friendly" practices including accelerating courses and degrees for service members; free personal computers; looser prerequisite requirements; and abundant credit transfers.

For example, at the University of Phoenix members of the US Armed Forces can earn an associate's degree by taking a single five-week online class in written communications and then making up the other nineteen required courses by giving credits for courses taken elsewhere in the student's military experience coupled with earning passing grades on tests in specific subject areas.

The online programs also have been adept at charging tuition at precisely the maximum rate reimbursed for the military by US taxpayers, meaning that service members do not have to pay *any* out-of-pocket tuition. This pricing strategy enables the for-profit online schools to compete very effectively against even public-funded community colleges that offer classes on a military basis for as little as $50 a credit. In anyone's math, free beats $50. As a result, the vice president for outreach at the University of Oklahoma, once the leading provider of graduate degrees to the US military, predicted that a decade from now we may not find traditional public or private universities involved in military education at all.

Despite the substantial recent progress made by providers of online learning in creating a favorable impression among corporate employers, issues like those arising in the active duty military programs have hampered more conclusive corporate acceptance of online learning credentials. When the 2008 *Vault.com* study asked employers if they would give equal consideration to job candidates with online degrees compared with degrees from traditional colleges, 63 percent still favored job candidates from the traditional sector and only 35 percent said they would give online graduates equal consideration. Obviously part of the reason for providing taxpayer benefits to active-duty military personnel is to help facilitate a smooth transition to civilian employment once the period of service ends. Any failure of online programs to provide education sufficient for "gainful employment" reflects poorly on the taxpayers' investment.

The US Department of Defense is aware that human resource executives at major companies are often reluctant to hire military graduates who have degrees from online programs from for-profit schools. Consequently, the DOD plans to subject online programs to further review by the American Council on Education, which already monitors face-to-face classes on military bases and is continuing to develop new standards for online learning.

It would be most helpful if the for-profit sector itself took steps–through the accreditation bodies where it has greatest impact–to "clean up its act" in terms of the abuses that have emerged, such as lightweight curricula and dubious student-recruiting practices (like marketing at homeless shelters). As will be discussed further in Chapter IV, the US Department of Education is actively considering norms and metrics to measure whether for-profit providers are in fact providing a level of education sufficient to assure that their graduates can attain "gainful employment" in return for the tuition rates charged.

Just as the online for-profit sector is facing new regulatory challenges to their highly successful business model, the traditional higher education sector is at last beginning to realize the vast potential of online learning.

Several categories of colleges and universities have led the relatively recent charge into Cyber education. Smaller private nonprofit institutions, including religiously affiliated colleges and universities, have grasped the online potential during the recent period of intensified competition and financial stress. They have taken steps to leverage their "legacy" investments in full-time faculty by reaching out to the adult-learner market, particularly with graduate programs that extend upward from their existing undergraduate offerings, delivered in whole or in part online.

Among the more successful private online operators is Touro University, a private nonprofit college based in New York City, which describes itself as a nonsectarian but Jewish-sponsored institution. In 1998 it founded a separate online division, Touro International University, which also served a large number of military personnel. Touro had long been active in outreach to working adults, operating campuses in California, Florida, Nevada, Berlin, Jerusalem and Moscow. In due course, Touro separately packaged and put its highly successful online college up for sale to generate proceeds to solidify its endowment. Touro International was particularly attractive as a sale candidate because of its accreditation by the Western Association of Schools and Colleges, one of the six regional accreditors accepted by the Department of Education as satisfactory for purposes of eligibility for federal financial assistance.

Regis College, a Jesuit university based in Denver, also rapidly expanded its online program through its School of Professional Studies. Regis was innovative in designing programs for working adults, particularly in terms of intensified or accelerated course schedules that typically are grouped in eight-week clusters that somewhat resemble the five- to nine-week course programs commonly associated with for-profit schools. Other Catholic liberal arts colleges around the country, such as Saint Mary's in

Moraga, California, have integrated online segments into their longstanding graduate business degree programs for working adults.

Some larger state-sponsored universities also have sought to carve out substantial niches in the online working-adult market to parallel those established by private institutions. University College of the University of Maryland is a prime example, and other schools have followed suit including such institutions as Central Michigan University. Results vary as traditional campuses wade into the realm of online education.

An ambitious "global campus" online initiative at the University of Illinois collapsed under the weight of faculty resistance to what was perceived as a University of Phoenix model for online teaching, with adjuncts and graduate assistants having the lion's share of student contact. But other large online programs at state institutions have thrived: U Mass Online, which pioneered a fully online MBA, enrolls an aggregate of nearly 50,000 students, earning the university $56 million in 2009; Penn State's World Campus has provided similar returns and includes a new online Doctor of Business Administration program. The University of Indiana created a new "Online University" having recognized the financial attractiveness of the working adult market by offering undergraduate degree-completion programs to residents of other states and even pricing those offerings at the favorable Indiana "in state" rate.

Several elite universities (including NYU and Stanford) with commitments to substantial adult-learning programs have generally segregated into schools of "Professional Studies" or "Extension Universities" (which may or may not offer full graduate degrees). Institutions such as Boston University, with significant continuing-education commitments serving a broad range of professional communities, have also made extensive use of online delivery.

Universities long associated with cutting-edge technology development, such as the Massachusetts Institute of Technology, have moved beyond basic Internet-delivery technology to provide digitized content not only online but via modularized delivery to mobile communication devices like MP3 players and iPhones. Hundreds of full college courses are available online on podcasts through MIT (for free) and via downloads from Apple's iTunes Store as well as through the facilities of Microsoft. Such delivery does not (yet) involve granting academic credit.

Another major expansion of online education will come through college e-textbooks, particularly with the development of both the Kindle digital book and the new Apple iPad. In 2009 the sales of printed college textbooks exceed $5 billion while e-text sales were merely $115 million, but expectations are that there will be a continuing push to make all higher education textbooks available in digital formats. The market for electronic learning products and services is projected to grow more than 7 percent over the next five years to $23.8 billion by 2014.

The explosion in online learning content has, of course, also created vast new opportunities for educational technology enterprises, particularly including the whole new industry that has arisen around "learning management systems." This phenomenon extends down through the K-12 level as more students are exposed to educational content online (thus embedding the "ed tech" expectation of the next generation of college students). The learning-management-system market initially formed around proprietary systems for managing online content, such as the independent public company Blackboard, the E-College system now owned by the global publishing firm Pearson, and the Angel system recently acquired by Blackboard.

More recently a host of new entrants have emerged based on so-called "open-platform" learning-management systems, such as Moodle, which is being adopted by a growing number of colleges and universities (including Golden Gate University) and Sekai, which has been taken up by schools with large, sophisticated technology-management centers of their own, such as the University of Michigan, Georgia Tech, and Louisiana State University.

A recent survey conducted through an initiative of the Western Cooperative for Educational Telecommunications and the Campus Computing Project revealed that organizational structures for managing and receiving online educational programs are in a state of flux. Approximately 45 percent of schools with online delivery restructured their management of those programs in the two years prior to 2009, and 52 percent anticipate that they will be restructuring in 2010-2011.

One of the main challenges in terms of managing online learning platforms is providing "24/7" technology support, as opposed to the traditional campus model of nine-to-five, Monday through Friday. Another challenge is to train the teaching faculty in online and podcasting technology. Only slightly more than half of the institutions surveyed reported that they had established mandatory online technology training programs for their instructors.

New lecture-capture video technologies reflecting the now-ubiquitous YouTube experience create online content directly from traditional in-person classroom lectures, even incorporating simultaneous and segmental feed-ins of PowerPoint presentations and other digital media. Further refinement of this technology opens the door to tremendous productivity enhancements in course delivery, with potential savings in instructional costs associated with using in-person and online content in interchangeable ways.

Social media networks such as Facebook, MySpace, and LinkedIn similarly offer a major opportunity to build a "virtual campus" experience for online learners. These can include social clubs built around career focus and academic specialties, and interchange information between students and faculty on content-sharing websites and software such as "wikis" and other specifically designed devices to enhance Cyber learning communities.

### Colleges must learn to do "more with less."

The dean of Boalt Hall, the law school of the University of California's select Berkeley campus, recently proposed opening an eleventh UC campus in a fully online format, as a potential long-term solution to the state's severe higher education budget constraints. As noted in Chapter I, Dean Christopher Edley has found support in this proposition from then-Governor Arnold Schwarzenegger's office, from UC President Mark Yudof (who ventured to Silicon Valley to present the idea to a group of technology executives), and from the UC Board of Regents. In an interview with the *Chronicle of Higher Education* published in July 2009, Edley said he had found that many transfer-ready students in community colleges in California were opting to attend the for-profit University of Phoenix instead of the University of California–especially African American and Latino/Chicano students. He hypothesized that they were doing so because of their ability to do coursework online while working part-time to put themselves through school–a model virtually perfected by the University of Phoenix.

California is serving only about 60 percent of the college-age cohort that its master plan contemplates. Edley suggested that the state could utilize private resources for the up-front investment in an online campus (just as the University of Phoenix did), either from donations or from investors who would front the capital in exchange for a return on net revenues. Edley found the faculty reaction to his proposal mixed, but cautiously supportive, with some thinking that professional master's degrees would be a more promising initial step than full-blown undergraduate offerings. He foresaw that to assure quality and reputation, the faculty leading such an online UC campus would have to be drawn from the core tenure-track, indistinguishable from the traditional faculty structure of the rest of the ten-campus system.

Even so, UC's online ambitions face some serious obstacles, according to a May 14, 2010 follow-up article in the *Chronicle of Higher Education*. In addition to UC's poor history of adopting online instruction, the *Chronicle* observed that: "Professors hold unusually tight control over the curriculum and many consider online a poor substitute for direct classroom contact. As a result, courses could take years to gain approval." UC has proposed a pilot project aiming to create online versions of about twenty-five high-enrollment entry-level undergraduate courses such as calculus, composition, organic chemistry and world history. The cost is anticipated to be about quarter of a million dollars on each such new online course with professors competing for grant money to build the classes, deliver the content and then evaluate the course. The pilot is being developed in 2011 with the first courses expected to be offered by January 2012.

Some UC Berkeley professors express the view that offering full online degrees would undermine the quality of the University of California undergraduate degrees and not really provide access to the UC research faculty. Others call the proposal "pie in the sky." Even so there are those who are particularly enthusiastic, seeing the proposal as enabling the UC system to utilize its faculty resources more effectively. Nonetheless, even Dean Edley isn't sure if the project will succeed. "What I fear," he said, "is that the coalition of willing. . .will be stopped dead in their tracks by the bureaucracy."

Whether or not Dean Edley, President Yudof and the Governor's office are right about the potential of online learning at the University of California, there's no question that online learning will play a central role in the university of the future, whether it is public, private or for-profit.

Nearly 12 million post-secondary students in the United States were taking some or all of their classes online by the end of 2009. Forecasts are that this number will expand to 22 million by 2014. According to estimates released by the research firm Ambient, by 2014 just slightly more than 5 million students will take all their courses in physical classrooms and more than 3.5 million will be taking all their classes online, while another 18 million will take at least some online classes.

A June 2009 study "The College of 2020: Students" published by the Chronicle Research Services predicted that universities which have resisted putting some of their courses online will almost certainly have to introduce online programs quickly to meet students' demand for more convenience. Students increasingly will expect access to classes from cellular phones and other portable computing devices, and will want to monitor classes online even if the classes are delivered in person. The Chronicle study also noted that colleges are under immense pressure to change quickly because of intensified scrutiny of their costs, as well as the pressures to adapt to instant access to information. Equally important are the next generation of college students who are currently enrolled in primary and secondary schools in more than two-thirds of the school districts have at least one student taking an online course.

Indeed, the study's research panel found that only about half of higher education institutions believe that in 2020 their enrollment will be primarily made up of traditional age full-time students. One-third of respondents expect that students could be taking up to 60 percent of their courses entirely online. Another 25 percent of survey respondents projected that students will take somewhere in the range of 20- to 40 percent of their courses online, and nearly 10 percent think that the percentage of online courses will be even greater.

Higher education leadership is not yet comfortable with their knowledge of how to "credentialize" student-driven learning, including online options, according to *Inside Higher Education*, which reported on remarks by a panel of college leaders at the TIAA-CREF Institute's 2010 Higher Education Leadership Conference. Nonetheless, budget considerations are driving them to consider shifting resources to support technology-driven learning platforms to meet the expectations of the upcoming generation of students.

The Chronicle report found that today's high school students–dubbed the "new millennials"–see their educational future built almost entirely around technology. Their vision of what they want from their education may well be criticized by traditional educators, but cannot be simply dismissed. These students will want it all–a variety of learning options that they can mix and match to play to their strengths. While the report found that some faculty members, administrators and academic deans continue to view online coursework as "anathema," it concluded that "nothing is as likely to change the face of higher education over the next decade as the switch to more online learning."

No longer is the venue limited to a classroom on campus, as illustrated in a November 4, 2010, report in *The New York Times* which included several anecdotes about students "learning in the dorms" because their classes are now being delivered on the Web, including at the universities of Florida, Iowa and North Carolina.

The Internet has truly "changed everything" (even higher education) by making information available on a moment's notice to anyone seeking it. At the end of the day, the challenge for all colleges will be to provide a multitude of options simultaneously, with enough flexibility to evolve even more to adapt to changing markets.

The challenge for state-sponsored and private nonprofit universities will be whether they will continue to cede further ground to the for-profit institutions, which have proved to be adept both at focusing on their customers *and* in obtaining an extraordinary degree of covert US taxpayer support.

Chapter IV
# TAXPAYER U

"The art of taxation consists in so plucking
the goose as to obtain the largest amount
of feathers with the least amount of hissing."
Jean-Baptiste Colbert

The US taxpayer has unwittingly and foolishly been the lead under-writer in the tremendous growth of the for-profit higher education sector, bearing most of the downside risks with few upside rewards. Over the past three decades, for-profit colleges have designed a business model that enabled enrollment to climb at six times the rate of other American universities.

While our future economy will need at least 40 percent of its citizens to have college degrees, we are producing graduates at a rate of less than 30 percent of the population—and taking six years to do so. To their credit, the for-profit institutions have made progress in addressing the nation's "graduation gridlock" (described in Chapter II) by catering to working-adult students, unlike traditional universities which have made only modest efforts to accommodate these nontraditional students.

For-profits thrived by upending the long-standing operating model of universities. They treat higher learning as a business, students as customers and "college traditions" as disposable. To meet consumer demand, they offer year-round schedules and online degree programs that are con-

venient for working adult students and their families. They have central-
ized course design and utilize cost-efficient part-time instructors. The for-
profits have attracted substantial equity investment by their willingness to
innovate, as well as by the peculiar dynamics of tuition pricing (annual
increases for essentially the same 'product'). More importantly, their healthy
operating margins are substantially underwritten by federal student-loan
programs that shift the credit risk from shareholders to the taxpayer. From
my years on Wall Street, I know full well how the markets appreciate this
kind of risk-free reward.

For-profit postsecondary education has been around since the middle
of the nineteenth century, when it emerged as virtually the only provider of
instruction in the then-new field of bookkeeping. From the Civil War through
the early decades of the twentieth century, for-profit institutes expanded
to cover accounting and a focus on general business education–a subject
that had been largely avoided by traditional universities–as well as a variety of vocational career tracks from beautician to auto-body maintenance,
which required special training but not college degrees.

Just a few decades ago, only about 100,000 students attended for-
profit colleges, and the sector was primarily a field of privately owned,
regional businesses that focused on fields like cosmetology, food preparation and office services. These for-profits concentrated on serving work-
ing-class adults who needed skills for better paying jobs but couldn't take
time off from work to attend class in a traditional education setting. The
for-profits gained a small foothold to grow in a degree-granting direction
with the passage of the GI Bill after World War II.

Today's for-profit colleges have aggressively expanded their mission
to the associate, bachelor's, and advanced professional degree fields,
with more than 90 percent of their enrollment attributable to these degree
programs. The strong growth was made possible by the for-profit schools
obtaining accreditation, which in turn qualified their students for a broad

range of student loans and grants, and further fueled by their abili
into the public equity markets when investors recognized that tra
colleges and universities were failing to serve the unmet needs of working
students.

As we've seen in Chapter I, both public and private nonprofit schools
remained largely wedded to traditional academic calendars and delivery
systems that proved a discouragingly high barrier to those students who
could not afford to attend college without working at least part time, or
older students who had dropped out of the education system directly after
high school and were seeking to return despite full-time work and family
obligations. The discouraging statistics (shown in Chapter II) regarding
the failure of college matriculants to complete degrees was seen as an
opportunity by for-profit educational entrepreneurs and their equity investors. Investors were also attracted to the education sector by a situation many other industries would be delighted to enjoy: higher education
consumers are *already conditioned* to pay higher tuition pricing every
year for essentially the same product, regardless of whether it is "new and
improved." If you can cut production cost, commoditize the product and
optimize delivery, this kind of market can be a bonanza.

Before examining the core elements of the for-profit model, let's review just how powerful that model has become. Enrollment in the nearly
3,000 for-profit career colleges in the US has grown by an average of 9
percent a year over the past thirty years, compared with only 1.5 percent
growth for all institutions. For-profit schools now educate about 10 percent of the roughly 18 million students who attend American degree-granting
institutions annually. In 2010 the University of Phoenix, the largest for-
profit school, passed the California State University system as the second
largest system of higher education in the country, enrolling nearly a half
million students in 2010, surpassed only by the State University system of
New York.

These surging enrollments also have driven extraordinary hiring of faculty (both full time and part time), support staff and executives. *Inside Higher Education*, citing federal data from the National Center for Education Statistics, reported that the sector had double-digit percentage growth, to the extent that 50 percent of total higher education was accounted for by for-profit colleges and universities.

An extensive February 2010 article in the *Chronicle of Higher Education* catalogued how this rapidly expanding sector is attracting students who might otherwise have attended community college or public and private four-year institutions. The article quoted the president of a higher education consulting group as concluding that for-profits are "clearly a threat for both public and privates schools. . .especially for adult students returning to get a BA or going part time to get a master's."

State institutions and small private schools are attempting to make up for tuition shortfalls by boosting enrollments of adult students–especially in such reputed "cash-cow" fields as graduate business education. Traditional schools, though, are forced to compete head-to-head with for-profit institutions but without the benefit of their highly efficient business models, much less the private equity and federal loan support that underwrites the for-profits' massive marketing programs.

The for-profit sector is dominated today by thirteen publicly traded corporate universities; the largest is the Apollo Group and its flagship University of Phoenix, which manages 200 campuses in thirty-nine states, Canada, Mexico, The Netherlands, Puerto Rico, and the U.K. Its growth has been supercharged by students who attend classes primarily online. UP enrollment is larger than each of the other twelve for-profit higher education firms, which range in enrollment from 35,000 to 136,000 students. Here are the "Top Ten" according to the *Chronicle of Higher Education*:

| | Fall 2009 Enrollment | Percent Growth over 2008 | Brand Names or Core Niches |
|---|---|---|---|
| Apollo Group | 443,000 | 22.3 % | University of Phoenix |
| Education Management Corporation | 136,000 | 22.7 % | Argosy University; Art Institutes |
| Career Education | 113,900 | 18.6 % | Le Cordon Bleu; American InterContinental University |
| DeVry | 101,648 | 37.1 % | DeVry: IT and business; Caribbean medical school |
| Corinthian | 93,493 | 25.9 % | Heald College Colleges, |
| ITT Education Services | 79,208 | 28.7 % | ITT Technical Institutes; Daniel Webster College |
| American Public Education | 55,300 | 42.2 % | American Military University |
| Bridgepoint Education | 54,894 | 79.7 % | Ashford University |
| Strayer Education | 54,317 | 21.9 % | Strayer Online |
| Grand Canyon Education | 34,218 | 55.8 % | Christian; online |

At a time when public and private nonprofit colleges and universities are cutting budgets, staff, faculty, classes, programs and student resources, and still barely breaking even or losing money, how is it that the for-profit sector is growing, thriving and making money? Don't the for-profits have to account not only for the costs of delivery of educational services, but also generate sufficient margins to pay corporate taxes and generous returns for their investors?

Actually, that is a task they have accomplished exceedingly well.

The reasons for the success of the for-profit business model are numerous, but can be broken down into ten categories of strategy and tactics, starting with the fundamental premise that *education can and indeed should be organized and operated like a business.*

## 1. Treating college as a business and students as customers

A common tenet of strategy theory, taught in the best traditional business schools, is that success starts with identifying an unmet customer need in the marketplace. In the case of US higher education, the unmet need is that of students who need to work while attending school, if only to afford levels of tuition that have grown well beyond the rate of inflation. Given the rising tuition pricing of recent years, it seems clear that traditional colleges and universities have both *created* the unmet need by raising tuition repeatedly, and then *failed to respond* to it by abandoning any real sense of mission to provide broad-based access to educational opportunity–a colossal strategic error.

One reason traditional universities failed to respond to the needs of working students was the reluctance of many academics to recognize students as "customers." Doing so would have led them to focus on student needs as a primary organizing principle, but to many traditional faculty members, the term "customer" often has a pejorative connotation, as someone who is to be "exploited to their disadvantage." This view goes along with a negative view of "business" generally held by many in academia, as though the main objective of any for-profit business is simply to exploit individuals, rather than respond to an unmet market need.

From that viewpoint, some traditional school leaders take a posture of moral superiority in their disdain for a "customer-centric" educational structure, viewing "students" as a special category of consumer who need to be *protected* by those who know best what is good for them. Unfortunately these academics misunderstand the premise of successful business operations–the fact that serving customer need is the central focus of the business-value calculus. For-profits have structured their educational offerings to at least *appear* to respond to the needs of their customers. When they forget this principle and in fact exploit their student-customers (as well as the American taxpayer), they threaten to kill their "golden goose," as we shall see later in this Chapter.

## 2. Building academic structure from scratch

It is another axiom of business strategy that, once an unmet market need is identified, a successful organization will shape its structure, allocate its resources, and define its objectives to meet those needs better than others. The organization must develop a "distinctive competence" in serving its customers in a manner that creates a "win-win" relationship: competitive advantage and profits for the business, and for the customer, consistent value for money spent.

For-profit colleges and universities by their very nature do not carry with them the traditional academic structures that have stood in the way of the ability–or willingness–of public and private universities to respond with alacrity to the needs of student-customers who work while pursuing their studies. When it came to designing their postsecondary degree programs the for-profits had the advantage of starting with a clean slate. They did not have the baggage of academic systems or faculty governance that elevates academic policy (and teacher influence or control) over business-model considerations in designing and shaping curricula and delivery modalities.

The for-profit sector also achieved a distinct competitive advantage by throwing out the traditional but antiquated September-to-May academic calendar in favor of operating in cycles geared to contemporary life of working adults and the annual federal financial aid cycle (with its own particularly flexible definition of "academic year"). The path to degree completion designed by the for-profits was organized around students' ability to attend classes with maximum financial and work/life efficiency *and* to obtain maximum federal financial aid. Instead of the traditional "start in the fall," the teaching calendar was set up to serve customers "any time, anywhere"–a now-common posture of successful businesses in our globalized economy.

The for-profits also re-examined the question of what an ideal course length would be in terms of student learning. Focusing on traditional measures of learning efficiency like absorption and retention of knowledge, they found that course lengths far shorter than the traditional fifteen- to seventeen-week semester system term (and its equivalent ten- to twelve-week quarter term) could actually be at least as effective, if not more so, in terms op imparting knowledge. This finding, which became the basis for the for-profits' academic cycle, led to the related discovery that adult students are often better at learning and retaining material "one course at a time." Together, these two insights fostered a new academic program structure starting at multiple times of the year, and proceeding through a set of individual courses focused in cycles of five- to nine-weeks, sequenced all the way to completion.

Gregory O'Brien, an administrator with long experience in traditional higher education, explains how the for-profit sector's innovations changed the old ways of designing the teaching calendar. "On traditional campuses the focus is on faculty," O'Brien observed. "At for-profit institutions, students are the Number one concern." He cites a case where a senior, tenured faculty member would only teach on certain days, and the university complied. Not true at for-profits. There, O'Brien says, "faculty members teach courses established by the university at times that work best for students."

## 3. Discarding "faculty governance" but winning academic accreditation

In order to establish flexible academic cycles and class schedules, the management of for-profit universities moved the responsibility for academic planning away from the "faculty-centric" model based on traditional notions of faculty governance of all curricular matters. It helped that the for-profits were "born free" of the traditional faculty structure of tenure-track professors moving through peer evaluations of their teaching and services and teaching faculty serving as department chairs holding tight to how curricula are organized and delivered.

For-profits simply avoided the tenure-track system for a business-like "employment-at-will" arrangement for instructors and staff in which programs and courses are identified and designed based on perceived market needs, and supervised by full-time curricular designers and administrators who work on a standardized (but not tenured) contractual system. Courses and programs are taught to a template relatively free of individual faculty idiosyncrasies.

A further major step away from traditional academic structures, pioneered at the for-profit leader University of Phoenix, was to abandon the traditional amount of student-instructor contact time for the typical three-credit semester (or quarter) course: forty- to forty-five contact hours of instructor face time in classroom lectures or other direct presentational or discussion activity with students.

In the University of Phoenix model, up to 50 percent of traditional instructor time may be replaced by scheduled projects required to be undertaken by the students themselves *without* the presence of a teacher. The University of Phoenix convinced its accreditor (the Higher Learning Commission of the North Central Association of Colleges and Schools) that the work required of students in these group projects was equivalent to direct contact with a professor in terms of academic outcomes. *Nice work if you can get it!*

A related innovation pushed aggressively by for-profit institutions awards academic credit for "prior learning experience," including experience relating specifically to career-focused academic degree programs. It is obviously harder to claim that a structure with half-time instructor presence is deficient once it has been agreed that full academic credit can be earned with no professor present at all.

Despite these departures from traditional academic norms, gaining approval by one of the six regional accreditations bodies recognized by the US Department of Education was critical to the success of the for-profit sector. Accreditation allows the for-profits to participate in federal higher education aid programs–their life blood. Financial aid not only funds massive marketing campaigns, but also creates gigantic profits, all with taxpayer funding. Achieving accreditation was, not surprisingly, a long and bumpy road for the for-profit sector. In the 1960s and 1970s, several court cases tested the refusal of traditional accreditation bodies to even consider for-profit institutions. After meeting resistance from its "home" regional accreditor (the Western Association of Schools and Colleges) the University of Phoenix ultimately achieved accreditation after moving to Arizona, a region where accreditation policies were more flexible. As a result the University of Phoenix ultimately helped establish a national body that has only until recently served as a recognized accreditor for a range of other large for-profit universities.

The flexible "credit-hour" interpretation that is central to achieving for-profit accreditation, however, has lately come up for renewed assessment in connection with the US Department of Education's review of for-profit education issues. Citing abuse by some schools and accreditors, the Department of Ed has proposed for the first time a federal rule defining a "credit hour", and obligating accreditation agencies to assure that colleges are requiring enough work from students to justify the award of course credits. The department's inspector general had questioned relatively loose credit-hour policies in place at certain accrediting agencies. But the department also recognized that a hard and fast, purely numeric, traditional "seat time" calculation of a credit hour could inhibit legitimate innovation.

The proposed DOE rule takes both views into account. First it defines a credit hour in traditional terms as "one hour of classroom or direct faculty/student interaction and a minimum of three hours of out-of-class school work each week for approximately fifteen weeks for one semester or trimester hour of credit" (and the equivalent for quarter systems). But the proposed rule would also allow an exception keyed to "reasonable equivalence for an amount of work required in the main definition as referenced by learning outcomes and verified by evidence of student achievement." Review of credit-hour practices has heretofore been left to self-policing by the schools and their accreditors. In the future, if the proposed DOE norm is adopted, for-profits will face closer accreditation scrutiny in respect to demonstrating learning achievement where faculty "face time"–whether in-person or online–is cut to the bone.

More broadly, the regional academic accreditors may find themselves in the same awkward position as the three major credit rating agencies in the aftermath of the great financial defaults of 2007-2008. Like their financial world counterparts, the accreditors failed to catch deceptive marketing and loan-related practices (detailed later in this chapter) at for-profit institutions. This is particularly troublesome given that the accreditors, like the rating agencies, are officially recognized "gatekeepers" for federal education benefits. Just as rating-agency approval is required for SEC-registered public debt offerings, accreditation is required to make a school's students eligible for federal financial aid in the form of grants and loans. And it is the ability to access these federal dollars that in turn has fueled the explosive growth of for-profit enrollment online.

### 4. Seizing "first-mover advantage" online

The current generation of publicly traded for-profit universities also had the business sense to exploit the Internet for course and degree delivery from the get-go, as shown in Chapter III. A generation of equity investors previously hooked on the dot-coms was intrigued by a new model of a knowledge-based industry that would use Web-based technology to deliver its product. The for-profit sector exploited an opportunity to serve unmet needs in higher education that traditional colleges and universities had not only failed to recognize but in many ways had actively resisted and disparaged. Stock market investors shared no such reluctance. Investor equity was particularly useful in terms of the up-front costs tied to creating online curricula and offerings to produce educational outcomes that accreditors, who are particularly sensitive to new online offerings, would deem acceptable.

But the real payoff for the for-profits online offerings came in 2006 when Congress lifted the prohibition against providing federal financial aid for programs that were delivered more than 50 percent online. The increase in online enrollment at the for-profits since that "deregulation" has been extraordinary by any measure—particularly because it generated a huge windfall of additional, risk-free federal aid dollars.

### 5. Charging what the taxpayer will bear

Armed with fully accredited undergraduate- and graduate-degree programs, the for-profits focused on honing their mostly online instruction product to match their targeted tuition price-points that were positioned midway between the relatively low rates charged by state schools for in-state students but well below tuition charged at the elite private universities. Their pricing was deliberately designed to procure the maximum amount of federal education grants and loans for students attending part-time in real-world terms but who were considered full-time students by federal aid eligibility rules.

For example, one version of the federal "loan year" is composed of any consecutive period of thirty weeks of classes. The traditional semester-based system of two fifteen- to seventeen-week terms per calendar year (with summers off or on short session) fills the bill, as does the traditional ten- to twelve-week, three-a-year quarter system. But what for-profits quickly figured out was that a structure of monthly, eight-week or even five-week courses could be arranged to generate *more* than one year's worth of federal loan eligibility during a single calendar year as long as the school keeps enrollment open year round with entry points at various times of the students' own choosing.

The ability of for-profits to maximize their financial returns from pricing power that optimized federal aid dollars was greatly enhanced by a second key act of deregulation. During the Bush Administration, Congress also lifted the ceiling on the aggregate tuition revenue that could be funded by federal education aid from 75 percent to 90 percent. This change was an open invitation to the for-profits to price their offerings so as to generate almost all their income from the US taxpayer. Hunting season was open! By 2008, the College Board reported that, despite enrolling only 10 percent of higher education students, for-profits were accounting for 25 percent of federal Pell grants and student loans. According to a report released by the US Senate Health, Education and Labor Committee in June 2010, the five largest for-profit schools reported that federal education dollars comprised on average more than 77 percent of their 2009 revenue. In reality, the federal share is even higher because of certain exclusions from the calculations.

At for-profit universities 96 percent of students use loans to pay for school, compared to 72 percent at private nonprofit colleges and 64 percent at four-year public colleges. According to the College Board, for-profit graduates with a bachelor's degree carry an average indebtedness of $33,000–$13,000 more than public-college graduates and $5,000 more than those finishing at private colleges. For 2008-2009, the top three recipients of federal student aid were Phoenix, DeVry and Kaplan–all for-profit universities. Along with increasing student loan burdens, however, have come ever-larger profits for the for-profit sector: up 81 percent on average for 2001 through 2009.

For a snapshot that neatly captures just how successful the federal-aid-driven business model of the publicly traded for-profits has been since the new 90 percent federal source standard was enacted, consider the first-quarter 2010 filing with the US Securities and Exchange Commission of Bridgepoint Education, the parent company of Ashford University, a for-profit which began operations in 2005, the year of "deregulation." By March 31, 2010, it had amassed more than 65,000 students and 99 percent attend exclusively online. During the first quarter of 2010, Bridgepoint generated revenues of $156 million, an 85 percent increase year-over-year. And of that amount, $44 million or 28 percent was spent on marketing and promotion; just 25 percent or $39 million was spent on actual instructional costs and related services; and $50 million came down as operating income, up from $7 million in the same quarter of the year before, a 32 percent operating margin. (We will examine the implications for the taxpayer of this rather counter-intuitive ratio later in this chapter.)

Ashford University concentrates on four-year degree programs, so it is delivering services in the same market as the vast majority of nonprofit higher educational institutions. Unlike those other institutions, though, the university (and its parent company Bridgepoint) receives about 90 percent of its revenues from federal government sources. In 2009, 86 percent of Ashford revenue came from the Department of Education's Title IV higher education financing programs, and another 4 percent from federal programs assisting active-duty members of the military as well as veterans.

Ashford is hardy unique. Revenues at major for-profit colleges are generally about 75-to-90 percent tuition-driven, and most for-profits, like Bridgepoint's Ashford, operate as close to the legal limit of 90 percent revenue dependence on federal education aid as they can. Many would exceed even that high percentage of tuition reimbursements if the US military were included (more on the for-profits military focus later in this chapter).

As a consequence, as the columnist John Dizard pointed out in a May 22, 2010 article in *The Financial Times*, income statements at Bridgepoint and other for-profit schools have come to resemble the type of dependence on the government outlays typically associated with defense contractors. Lockheed Martin, for example, received 85 percent of its sales revenue from the US government in 2009, but its operating margin amounted to a little less than 10 percent; Bridgepoint's margin was three times that size. According to figures cited by the *Chronicle of Higher Education*, operating margins at publicly traded for-profit colleges averaged 21 percent in 2009 compared with the long-term S&P 500 average of 6 percent. Take it from a business school dean with Wall Street roots, the equity markets love this kind of "beat the Street" financial performance, especially when the risk of loss from student defaults on their loans is borne by the American taxpayer, not the shareholders.

## 6. Winning by default

As a matter of fact, students at for-profit schools are far more prone to default than students at other institutions of higher learning. With just 10 percent of higher education enrollment, for-profits attract 25 percent of federal aid dollars, but account for 44 percent of loan defaults (not including students who have been granted "extensions" or "forbearance" on their loans). The federal government has maintained these statistics on default rates two years out from when students leave school in order to enforce a rule barring financial aid eligibility for students at schools with default rates exceeding 25 percent. Concerned by a DOE Inspector General report that questioned the implications of focusing only on two-year default rates, Congress mandated in 2008 that three-year default rates be calculated and raised the bar on the "penalty box" to 30 percent, effective in 2014. This data, published in 2009, showed default rates at for-profit schools climbing toward 25 percent at those offering associates degrees, and to 18 percent at schools offering a BA degree or higher.

For-profits tend to cater to underserved and economically disadvantaged sectors of the populace and students need to borrow far more to pursue degrees at for-profit institutions than at state-supported colleges. Average annual tuition at for-profits was $14,000 in 2009, compared with $2,000 at community colleges and $7,000 for in-state students at public four-year universities. For-profit colleges have higher default rates—and drop out rates—as much as three times the rate at public universities. Of the twenty degree-granting colleges that would be disqualified if the pending 30 percent default threshold were in force in 2010, seventeen were for-profit colleges, according to the *Chronicle of Higher Education*.

Terrified that its three-year default rates could exceed the 30 percent threshold by the effective date of 2014 (which would put the schools out of business), the sector has taken rather unusual steps to mitigate that risk.

Some have resorted to dubious tactics utilizing debt-management companies and detective agencies to locate students who are having problems repaying their loans and then counseling them regarding seeking forbearance. Forbearance delays payments for six to twelve months and is reportedly "a piece of cake" to get. The *Chronicle* also reported that some default-management companies are even suggesting that for-profit colleges convince student borrowers to provide contact information for friends or relatives they'd like to invite to commencement, so that the schools can later use that information to get back in touch with former students about unpaid loans should the need arise.

Loan defaults are truly a tragedy of the first order for students, especially for those who don't complete their degree, or who only pile on interest if they are led to seek "forbearance" by agents of schools that are trying to stay in business by keeping their default rates down. As we saw in Chapter II, those who default on student loans may have their wages and tax refunds garnished by the government, lose their credit standing, and be denied mortgages, car loans, credit cards, and even rental apartments and jobs. But defaults are also a tragedy for the US taxpayer over the longer term. The same *Chronicle of Higher Education* study revealed previously unpublished Department of Education data showing that fifteen years into repayment after leaving school, two of every five loans– 40 percent–made to students at two-year for-profit schools were in default.

While equity markets have from time to time punished the for-profit higher education sector because of loan-default issues, in general their stock prices rise again if regulatory pressure is perceived to relent. Such has been the case with the ebb and flow of debate on the degree of enforcement of the federal requirement that these colleges provide learning outcomes that enable graduates to find the requisite "gainful employment" sufficient to pay off their loans. The stocks were pummeled when it first appeared that the Obama Administration would propose an across-the-board requirement that all for-profit colleges track whether the jobs obtained by their graduates were providing salaries equal to 8 percent of student debt. When the proposed rules were officially published, however, the for-profit stocks rallied in response to what turned out to be more nuanced norms that would set up three categories of "stress test" metrics regarding the relationship between gainful employment, default rates and continued eligibility for federal aid. However, the metrics for the first time would be assessed with actual salary data specific to the schools, rather then generic figures published by the Bureau of Labor Statistics. And importantly, "forbearance" arrangements would be counted as defaults, reducing the temptation for schools to entice former students into "work-out" arrangements that would saddle them with even more indebtedness down the road.

**Proposed DOE Gainful Employment Rules for**

**Federal Education Aid Eligibility**

**Graduates' Debt Burdens**

| | | (A) | (B) | (C) |
|---|---|---|---|---|
| | | **ABOVE 12 % of Total Income AND 35 % of Discretionary Income** | **BELOW 8 % of Total Income OR 20 % of Discretionary Income** | **Neither (A) nor (B)** |
| **Percent of Aggregate Loan Principal Repaid Four Years Out by Former Students (Graduates and Drop-outs)** | **Above 45 %** | **Fully Eligible** | **Fully Eligible** | **Fully Eligible** |
| | **35 % to 45 %** | **Restricted** | **Fully Eligible** | **Restricted** |
| | **Below 35 %** | **Ineligible** | **Fully Eligible** | **Restricted** |

Source: Adapted from a chart published by the *Chronicle of Higher Education*

DOE officials projected that if the proposed new rules scheduled to take effect in 2012 were operative in 2010, about 5 percent of for-profit schools would be inline to lose eligibility, 55 percent would face restrictions on their enrollments, and only 40 percent would remain fully eligible with no mandate for change. Enrollments at restricted programs would be held to no more than the average of the prior three year totals–meaning these schools could not grow until they became fully compliant. Schools would have one year to reduce their tuition pricing or improve their job placement before eligibility would be revoked. DOE estimated that 50 percent of the for-profits could assure compliance by cutting tuition 10 percent.

For-profit advocates argue that the proposed rules amount to *de facto* price controls that will stifle innovation. But critics of for-profits such as Senator Tom Harkin of Iowa observed that "allowing a school to continue to walk away with taxpayer dollars" if only 35 percent of its students can pay off their loans is a "case of shockingly low expectations."

In truth, problems by the for-profit sector posed for US taxpayers go well beyond the issue of excessive loans defaults. Pending the finalization of metrics for applying the "gainful employment" rule, the Department of Education issued new reporting rules applying to all college degree programs at for-profit schools, requiring an annual statement for each program of:

- Total annual enrollment;
- The identity of each student who enrolls;
- The completion date for each student who finished;
- The amount of loans each completer received from the school itself; and
- Evidence of whether students moved on to a higher level program at the same school or another.

The first such reports are required to be submitted by October 2011, covering the four academic years beginning with 2006-2007.

In addition, for each program subject to gainful-employment requirements, the institution must provide prospective students with all of the following disclosures:

- The names and Standard Occupational Classification (SIC) codes for the occupations that the program prepares students to enter;
- The on-time graduation rate for students completing the program (dividing the number of students who completed the program within normal time by the total number of students who completed the program);
- The tuition and fees assessed for completing the program within normal time, the typical costs for books and supplies (unless those costs are included as part of tuition and fees), and the cost of room and board, if applicable;
- The placement rate for students completing the program, as determined under a methodology developed by the National Center for Education Statistics (NCES), when that rate is available; and
- The median loan debt incurred by students who completed the program.

The institution must also include these disclosures in promotional materials and on its websites. The schools are mandated to provide the disclosures in a simple and meaningful manner on the home page of its program website, providing a prominent and direct link on any other web page containing general, academic, or admissions information about the relevant program to the single website page that contains all the required information.

Finalization of the metrics proposed by the Department of Education that would define gainful employment in terms of repayment rates and debt-to-income measures, however, was delayed until early 2011, for implementation by mid-2012.

## 7. Driving enrollment with taxpayer-funded marketing power

As exemplified by Bridgepoint's Ashford University, about 25 percent of for-profit colleges' government-subsidized tuition revenue is spent on aggressive student-recruitment programs. Taxpayers are financing not just educational expenditures but expensive advertising campaigns and high-pressure call centers as well. The University of Phoenix spends nearly $1 billion annually on promotion, including using its federally subsidized profits to purchase naming rights to a sports stadium. As noted previously, Bridgepoint Education actually spent 28 percent of this year's first-quarter revenue on promotion, compared with only 25 percent spent on instruction costs and services!

Imagine taxpayers' reactions if traditional schools (which receive a much lower level of their funding from federal student grants and loans) decided to divert a quarter of their already constrained budgets away from the classroom to carry out massive self-promotion campaigns. Surely the taxpayer is not intending to subsidize the for-profits' ability to provide "gainful employment" primarily for the advertising industry! But that seems to be more and more the case.

A 2006 study by Samuel C. Woods, a lecturer at Stanford University, outlined how dramatically both income and expenditure patterns differ between nonprofit and for-profit colleges. According to Woods, the for-profits depend on tuition for 93 percent of their revenue, making them utterly dependent on generating ever-increasing enrollment linked to federal aid dollars. With materially lower *instructional* costs than the other types of higher-education institutions, the for-profits can expend a substantially larger percentage of their budgets on student recruiting and related advertising expenses. At for-profits that amounts to 23 percent of revenues per-year on average, compared with only 1-to-2 percent for the typical nonprofit public or private colleges, Woods also notes. "They are going to spend the money on getting you. And once they have you, it's like you are an acquired annuity." He observes that the for-profits have more in common with a health club than a university because of the way they devote themselves to student acquisition and retention.

For-profit schools clearly have a lot more marketing money at their disposal than other universities. For the three months ended November 30, 2000, Apollo (Phoenix's parent company) spent $275 million on selling and promotion, a pace of $1 billion a year. Indeed, there is an eerie resemblance between the sub-prime mortgage industry and the for-profit schools not just in their common history of loan defaults, but also their sophisticated telephone sales centers and expensive marketing programs.

A 2010 *Chronicle of Higher Education* article described the sector's telephone marketing culture, designed to "take prospective students off the market" as soon as the first contact: "If you express an interest today at a for-profit, you will get a phone call from someone within fifteen minutes, and that person will work with you to complete your application and figure out what program makes sense for enrollment starting the next month," explains John Katzman, chief executive of 2tor. Some for-profits seek to drive all prospective student inquiry directly to their call centers by rarely publishing actual class schedules or tuition rates on their websites. This simple tactic forces prospects to contact the schools by telephone, placing themselves at the mercy of the school's phone-sales operators.

Problems of marketing irregularities at for-profits appear to have spread from a few "bad apples" to a truly systemic issue, according to Senator Tom Harkin, who chairs the Senate Health, Education, Labor and Pension Committee. A 2010 Government Accounting Office undercover investigation of call-center recruiting practices at for-profit colleges, presented to Harkin's committee, revealed "fraudulent, deceptive or otherwise questionable marketing practices" at all fifteen schools under study, including direct inducements for fraudulent financial aid applications by prospective students at four schools.

Examples included financial aid officers who told undercover applicants not to report a quarter million dollars in savings specifically required to be disclosed on the DOE's financial aid form; one counselor stated that such information "was none of the government's business"! Another counselor encouraged an applicant to add a false number of dependents to the form. At other schools, false claims about institutional accreditation were made by administrators and counselors, as well as misleading claims about salaries in professions linked to particular degrees. At several schools, applicants were falsely told they could not have financial aid consultations until after they had signed up for courses and paid their application fees. Still another for-profit school provided direct assistance to undercover applicants in answering questions on the exam they had to pass to gain admission.

The disturbing ratio of marketing expenditures to instructional expenditures at some for-profit colleges–attractive as it may be to their equity investors–raises public policy questions reminiscent of recent issues surrounding health-insurance reform. The new federal health-care legislation mandates insurers to show they are spending 85 percent of premiums received on supporting actual medical care as opposed to closing general administrative expenses.

As federal and state governments work to hammer out the definitions that will set the terms for this rule, it may be useful for the Department of Education to give similar thought to defining the appropriate relationship between how much of their taxpayer-funded tuition for-profit schools should be allowed to be spent on marketing as compared with actual educational content and delivery. Likewise, the policy logic of the Obama

Administration's push to a system of "direct" student lending was to get the federal loan billions right into the hands of students instead of passing through a group of fee-hungry bankers. Should not the same principles apply to the for-profit sectors, who are raking off a massive chunk of the student-loan pie to support their own marketing and profit margins?

Spurred by the revelations about for-profit marketing practices revealed in the GAO's "secret shopper" investigation, Senator Harkin has requested data from each of the publicly traded for-profit universities (as well a number of privately-held for-profit schools), including specifically:

- Total dollars spent on advertising, including direct mail, telemarketing and admission-counselor staff expense;
- Faculty compensation;
- Executive compensation;
- Financial aid administration;
- Facilities, equipment and furnishings;
- Litigation exposure;
- Debt service; and
- Distributions to shareholders.

This data, once delivered, will be a treasure-trove for Wall Street securities analysts who have not had access to such detailed transparency in the data that the companies have chosen to disclose in their regular SEC filings. It will also reveal to the American taxpayers exactly how the loans they underwrite to fund for-profit tuition are being spent, and how the ratio of marketing-to-instruction expense compares with public and nonprofit private institutions.

The for-profit universities have succeeded in delivering commoditized instruction conveniently, but that convenience comes at customized prices. They sell this package with the surfeit of marketing and promotional resources made available by dropping the traditional faculty-centered instructional system and employing a "federal-aid friendly" (as well as work-friendly) academic calendar. It is as though the for-profits have removed half the toothpaste from the tube, packaged the remainder for more convenient "home delivery" and then used federally subsidized promotional resources to successfully sell the benefits of "toothpaste light"–at the same price as the full tube.

The for-profits also have kept the immense profits of their model for themselves and their shareholders, while transferring the related risks to the US taxpayer. If the subprime mortgage financial crisis taught us anything, it should be at least that this kind of separation of risk from reward is a particularly dangerous brand of economic alchemy.

Indeed, several investment commentators have come expressly to view the for-profit college industry as a clone of the subprime mortgage disaster zone, even in terms of the sector's shareholders! David Einhorn, a leading hedge-fund guru, who correctly predicted Lehman Brothers' financial debacle, specifically advised investors to "short" for-profit college stocks because of such similarities. Similarly, *Kiplinger Personal Finance* reported in November 2010 that no other industry "is more rocked by controversy today," with their stocks taking a "horrific beating," given all the bad news emanating from the US Senate and Department of Education investigations of student loan defaults and shady marketing practices.

Indeed, the price of shares of the University of Phoenix parent, Apollo Group, fell nearly 25 percent after word came out that the controversy could lead to a quarter-on-quarter drop in new enrollments of up to 40 percent. Stocks of other companies such as Strayer Education, IIT Educational Services and Corinthian College also fell to remarkably cheap market prices–as low as only three times trailing earnings, a level previously associated with the worst of banks at the height of the Great Recession! In the wake of these share price drops, the SEC has also requested share trading information from Apollo, including its policies related to sales made by senior executives during 2009 around the time that the Department of Education was beginning its investigation of student loan policies at the University of Phoenix.

## 8. Keeping up the body count

Aware of the regulatory consequences of excessive loan defaults, the for-profit schools have created early-warning systems to alert them to potential dropouts from their system (who will be most at risk for defaulting). Yet they nonetheless suffer a degree of customer "churn" in some cases much like the early providers of cell-phone services. This may be due to the fact that for-profits spend only half as much as traditional universities on intervention systems such as student services and support.

For-profits, however, clearly have helped place a new focus on student-retention services in the face of traditional systems' poor record with respect to degree-completion programs. The for-profits less than stellar performance in terms of student retention may be primarily a result of their lower level of resource commitment to the central function of instruction. In many respects, the long-term success of for-profits may depend on whether they will really put the customer first or just put *acquiring* the customer first.

Although the actual drop-out rate among for-profit college students is difficult to calculate, a report to the US Senate in July 2010 reached its own conclusion: three of the four schools reporting any data at all enrolled more new students over the course of the year than the total number of students at the start. One school started the period with 62,000 students, enrolled 117,000 new students, but ended with just 86,000 students. Understanding precisely what portion of these students actually finishes with degrees is important in determining the value of federal investment in student aid, not to mention the taxpayers. Quite obviously, students who fail to graduate are at the most risk of lacking sufficient "gainful employ-ment" to fund their loan obligations.

## 9. Full-court press on the military

As for-profit colleges and universities face increasing regulatory con-cerns focused on the revenue derived from US educational assistance programs, many know they would exceed the 90 percent limit on feder-ally owned tuition dollars if financial support provided to military person-nel and veterans counted. It does not; making this is a key reason why for-profits market their programs so heavily to active-duty armed forces and veterans.

A front-page article in the *New York Times* (March 14, 2010) ob-served that for-profits' military-education programs "have come at sub-stantial taxpayer expense while often delivering dubious benefits to stu-dents, according to academics and advocates for greater benefits and financial aid." Critics say for-profit schools exaggerate the value of their degree programs, selling soldiers on dreams of middle-class wages while setting them up for defaulting on untenable debts they cannot cover with the low-wage jobs that the degrees will actually qualify them for, if they even finish. Concerned about aggressive marketing techniques to the mili-tary and to the broader civilian market, the Obama Administration is con-sidering, in addition to the new rules on gainful employment and default ratios, regulations to tighten existing prohibitions against paying recruiters based on enrollment targets.

Many of these concerns originated from issues which first surfaced at the University of Phoenix several years ago. In 2004, a Department of Education review of Phoenix's compensation practices alleged that the university had set up a system "designed to mislead the Department of Education and to evade detection of its improper incentive-compensation system." The report said that Phoenix pressured its recruiters to enroll students who were academically unqualified while using federal financial aid as a "tool for closing the sale."

The DOE report also described "intimidation techniques" used by recruiting managers on subordinates who were not meeting targeted enrollment numbers. Poorly performing recruiters, for instance, were said to be ordered to work in a glass-enclosed area known as the "red room," where senior recruiters and managers "hovered over the unfortunate recruiters" monitoring the success or failure of their calls.

Ultimately, the University of Phoenix paid a multi-million dollar fine to the Department of Education to close the investigation. Around the same time, however, two former employees filed a separate lawsuit against Phoenix under the Federal False Claims Act, which allows individuals to assert claims of fraud against the US Government, in this case in connection with obtaining federal student aid dollars. The suit was originally thrown out by a federal district court, but in 2007 it was allowed to proceed to trial by the Federal Appeals Court for the Ninth Circuit.

This lawsuit was eventually settled for $78.5 million paid to the government and the attorneys of the two former University of Phoenix employees. The university, of course, did not admit any wrongdoing as part of the settlement, and the Department of Education agreed to take no further action against Phoenix in the matter. A lawyer for the plaintiffs observed, however, that the discovery process in the case would assist authorities in reframing regulations regarding incentive compensation, and that the size of the settlement would deter other for-profit institutions from violating the letter or the spirit of those rules.

## 10. Buying accreditation at distressed prices

The latest emerging example of controversy surrounding how for-profit colleges benefit thanks to the American taxpayer concerns the practice of "buying accreditation." In this scenario, a for-profit corporation acquires an accredited but down-on-its-luck private nonprofit university for the purpose of gaining broadened access to federal loan programs available only to accredited institutions.

"Now they're taking a new tack in the quest to expand," according to a March 2010 report in *Bloomberg/BusinessWeek*. The report explained that "By exploiting loopholes in government regulation and an accreditation system that wasn't designed to evaluate for-profit takeovers, they're acquiring struggling nonprofit and religious colleges–and their coveted accreditation. Typically, the goal is to transform the schools into online behemoths at taxpayers' expense." According to *Bloomberg/BusinessWeek* "for-profit education companies, including ITT Educational Services, based in Carmel, Indiana, and Laureate Education Inc., in Baltimore, have purchased at least sixteen nonprofit colleges with regional accreditation since 2004, according to corporate announcements and filings with the US Securities and Exchange Commission."

Under normal rules, winning accreditation can take up to five years, but for-profit institutions simply bought accreditation (by acquiring accredited nonprofit institutions) and used those same five years to grow enrollments funded by the federal student loan and grant programs. For example, at Grand Canyon University, a Christian college in Phoenix purchased by private-equity investors, enrollment soared to 37,700 by 2009–up from 1,500 when it was purchased in 2004–with 92 percent of the students taking classes online. Bridgepoint Education increased enrollment at two regionally accredited colleges it bought in 2005 and 2007 to 53,688 students–up from 400 combined–after converting the schools to fully online operations.

"Purchased accreditation" also opens the door to easier transfer of credits from the for-profits to traditional colleges and universities, a strong enrollment selling point. The Department of Education is considering whether these kinds of acquisitions have the effect of circumventing federal requirements that require "new" for-profit schools to wait two years to qualify for such programs. A late response is at least better than none.

These acquisitions are also renewing controversy about the standards used by regional accrediting bodies in assessing such purchases and their consequences. Essentially, the accreditors are treating them as mere changes in ownership rather than as distinctly new colleges despite the fact that the end result is often a complete change in the academic and operational model, particularly in the transition to mostly online enrollment. *Bloomberg/ BusinessWeek* described how this process works in practice: "For accreditation to continue once the college is sold, the buyer must promise not to change its mission, Steven Crow, former executive director of the Chicago-based Higher Learning Commission, the largest regional body, said, '…You know by month six they would come back to you with a new game plan.'"

Although the horse is already out of the Higher Learning Commission's barn, the largest regional accreditor in the nation finally amended its policy this past year. Buyers will now have to wait one to four years if a substantial change of mission is involved. It would have been better to have employed that rule before the purchased accreditation merry-go-round started. For example, consider the $20.8 million acquisition by ITT Education of debt-ridden Daniel Webster College. The college president and board agreed to the sale as a last resort to save the college and its students' ability to continue school and receive federal aid.

After promising to leave Webster's administrators in place, ITT dismissed twenty employees for duplication of functions that could be performed by corporate headquarters staff, changed the curriculum and faculty structure, ousted the Webster president and replaced him with an ITT executive, and then re-wrote the Webster Faculty's self-study report (a document required for accreditation). These actions, predictably, took the regional accreditor by surprise.

Meanwhile, ITT plans to open more Daniel Webster campuses introducing programs in accounting, education, and health services, and–like the many other examples of purchased accreditation–expanding the online offerings, which the *Chronicle of Higher Education* calls the "holy grail" of the for-profits. As distinct form the mythical original, however, the for-profits appear to have actually seized this truly potent sword.

The for-profits have clearly demonstrated "how to succeed in business in ten easy lessons" with substantial help from the US taxpayers. The challenge for-profits pose for traditional higher education is whether nonprofit institutions and state universities can adopt some of the for-profits' insights into new delivery models–including online–to meet student demand for greater convenience, while avoiding the slick and slithering tactics that have gotten the for-profits into trouble and into the public pocketbook.

It should be relatively easy for nonprofit institutions to put the roughly 25 percent of the for-profit budgets that go for taxes and shareholders' returns to work becoming more effective in support of *both* instructional quality and convenient delivery. Indeed, one private nonprofit that focuses on the adult learner market–National University–has adopted the for-profit model and greatly enhanced its enrollment as well as its quasi-endowment by aggressively deploying online degree offerings. It remains to be seen whether more traditional academic institutions will more broadly adopt online strategies to expand their outreach to the 85 percent of today's postsecondary students who do not fit the "Joe or Jane College" mold.

But this will only happen if American taxpayers wake up and realize that, in terms of expanding access to higher education, they don't need to pay Starbucks prices to enjoy a perfectly satisfying blend!

# Part Two: The View from the President's Office

Chapter V

# WAITING FOR GODOT

"Paradigms may have shifted while in flight."
Virgin America Airlines

Shortly after I became president of Citrus College in 1982, I took a night course. I wanted to learn how to use a personal computer. The course had several advantages. The instructor was excellent, the syllabus was accurate and, best of all, the course utilized "Mastery Learning." You could take the computerized tests whenever you felt you were ready. If you failed, you could go back and take a different version of the test again three days later. If you passed that section of material, you could go on to the next leg of the class. There was no required "seat time." You simply had to demonstrate that you had mastered the material.

But there were some large negatives. The first part of the course dealt with the history of the computer. Although that might be interesting to some, it was of no real value in learning how to use a computer. After all, do you need to know the history of the automobile or how the motor works to drive a car? The second five weeks were spent learning to use "key punch" technology. The problem with that approach was that the industry was rapidly moving away from "key punch." In effect, the college was teaching technology that was not going to be used on the job in the near future–or any future!

The last third of the course finally covered what I was seeking: word processing, graphs, charts, and spread sheets. Those sessions were right on the mark and I could do all three at amateur skill level when the class ended.

I am not sure how long it would have taken to alter that course had the president of the college not taken it and felt strongly that the course did not deliver what students needed or what employers expected. Because of the force of the president's office, the structure of the course was significantly altered. The time spent on the history of the computer was dropped. Our "key punch" machines were leased, so we returned them. The revamped course focused almost entirely on the skills of word processing, graphs, charts, and spread sheets. Reflecting on these events, I am sure we were "just teaching the course the way we had always taught it."

But the use of computers was about to become much more ubiquitous. Computers were becoming much more user-friendly, more powerful, much less expensive, and a basic part of everyday business. Those who could not use one in the future would be relegated, discarded, or just plain obsolete.

The need for change was clear in that Citrus College computer class. And change came swiftly. But the same story of needed change without such a swift response has humbled our national automobile industry, the nation's newspaper industry and many more sectors of the economy. There is a tendency to just keep on doing what you have always done or, as another way of avoiding reality, pretending that any change forced by circumstance is "one time only," as if we can hit the "pause button" on reality.

In July of 2010, the executive director of San Francisco's Caltrain made a decision to stop the Holiday Train run. For years, a non-passenger train decorated with 40,000 lights had taken Santa to various stations over two full days. But this year, because of needed economies, there would be no train. Spokesperson Christine Dunn explained that it was "not a permanent decision," and that they hoped it would be brought back at a later time.

In January 2010, the University of Hawaii reached a six-year deal with its Professional Assembly union. The union agreed to temporary pay reductions of 6.7 percent for eighteen months. The kicker? Underline the word "temporary." The agreement calls for pay raises of 3 percent in 2013 and 2014 and the amounts lost would be fully recovered over a three-year period.

Caltrain and the University of Hawaii were simply "Waiting for Godot."

And that posture characterizes American higher education today. As I boarded a plane to attend the Council of Independent Colleges (CIC) President's Institute in January 2010, I picked up an article written by the president of the CIC: "Preventing the Doom-Sayers from Shaping the Debate." As the former director of debate at Michigan's Albion College, it seemed to me that the article read like a "first negative" speech of a debate (a straight denial of any need for change.) Allowing for the fact that this CIC article was a pep talk to the association's members, let's take a look at the chain of logic.

Making a case that there is no need to abandon the traditional model for American college and university education, the article asserted that college demands "full engagement," and characterized part-time study and online education as "certainly better than no study at all," but unmistakably sub-par. The attitude toward part-time study was similar to that of Alfred Kelly, a history professor I had at Wayne State University back in the 1960s. One day after the mass lecture to some 200 of us, I gathered up my courage and stood in line to "have a moment" with him. When I mentioned that I was working thirty hours a week, his grey eyes glared at me, and he belittled me for working my way through college. "Unless you are a full-time student, you can't possibly get better than a 'C' in my course," he bellowed.

As a matter of fact, I *was* a full-time student, carrying the normal fifteen-credit academic load *and* working thirty hours a week. No difference to Kelly: he delivered his "C" as my final grade. But Kelley's statement was made fifty years ago. I am surprised to see that blanket baloney still being peddled in 2010.

No doubt thousands of others from traditional academia share that point of view. Some are well-known and most are well-meaning: Warren Bennis, for instance, pleaded not to let "cold cost-cutting endanger the American model of education" in an article last year saying that "the best system of higher education in the world can't be done on the cheap." But it isn't only a question of "what we currently have" vs. "on the cheap". There is legitimate fear that government will disinvest. It took the current fiscal crisis in the Golden State for the University of California San Francisco to design a restructuring plan that over three years could cut more than 500 positions and save more than $60 million. And UC Berkeley has suddenly discovered a way to save $75 million. That's only two examples in one state. Think what **the bloat factor** is on the national scale!

Our public higher education system can be compared in a truly meaningful way with holiday and special day gift cards. Why? Because in 2009, $5 billion of the money spent acquiring them will not be fully utilized. People lose or misplace them; they even forget they have them. There is **that** degree of economic waste in our national college and university system!

When you are getting more money every year, what is the incentive to be efficient? The Bennis argument is a forced choice "either/or." But take it from someone who has been there–**massive room** for economy in higher education exists without harming graduate quality. But thousands of faculty, administrators and staff who came up through the system and who practice the current American model of traditional higher education cling to the tired old university model.

Even University of Pennsylvania Professor Robert M. Zemsky (who may be the leading in-house voice for change in higher education) understands that "the history of American higher education is well supplied with reform movements that have gone nowhere." Still, he advocates change from *inside* the system and laments that there has been no "dislodging event" to make changing the prevailing paradigm possible.

Look around you, Dr. Z.: international competition, the online revolution, for-profit colleges, the 85 percent nontraditional student body *and* the Great Recession. "Dislodging events" all (what we call "disruptive change" in Chapter XII). And when combined, converge and compose a change agent force as strong as gravity. And these *external* forces, not the internal ones, are driving change.

Just as Henry Ford's dominance with the Model T passed into history, change is coming to higher education. It is coming with increasing force. And it is coming whether tertiary education is ready or not. Although there are numerous forces converging and forcing change in the structure of American higher education, none is as compelling as the Great Recession. That swift and powerful economic tsunami's worldwide impact and devastating aftermath will affect individuals, families, communities, local, state and federal governments, and higher education for years to come. Let's consider first the impact on the lives of people.

My mother and father lived through the Great Depression and as a result they carefully thought out each family expenditure. Cash was king. They never owned a credit card. They bought their cars and even their house with cash. Even with FDIC, my parents never fully trusted banks. (*Maybe they were right?*) When my dad passed away, my son Scott found $20 bills stuffed into tin cans, cookie jars and cereal boxes. My parents had even made sure their burial expenses were paid in advance. They had been badly burned by the Great Depression. It was not going to happen to them again.

They also lived through World War II. Thirty years after the war had ended, I called my mom to tell her I was traveling to Japan. What was just an item of information for me was much more than that for her. After a long silence, she asked in all sincerity, "Why are you going *over there*? We fought a war with *those people* you know."

Great Depressions and World Wars are "life-changing events"; they indelibly alter our attitudes, beliefs, values, actions and our lives for years to come. Over the last three years, new generations of Americans, who are much too young to have had firsthand experience with or bitter memories of the Depression, learned just how vulnerable they are. Millions lost jobs, savings, investments, even their homes. That bitter firsthand "castor oil" is now on the tip of their taste buds and the results etched into their memories. Since our economy is based 70 percent on consumer behavior, we can predict that long after the Great Recession, spending will be less and savings will be more. And investors will hedge their bets as well since the stock market lost half its 14,000 value by the spring of 2009. Cash may not be hidden in tin cans and cereal boxes, but a lot of it will be squirreled away somewhere, not out there churning in the economy.

As for state spending, it's in for several years of curtailment. According to the National Council of State Legislatures, for the first time in recent history, state spending has gone down for two years in a row–a total of 9 percent, and state revenues dropped almost 8 percent in FY 2009. Over the first half of FY 2010, states made more than $50 billion in cuts, yet shortfalls amounting to almost $30 billion remained in three dozen states. And this situation is far from over. The NCSL anticipates $84 billion in shortfalls for FY 2011. Two in three states expect budget shortfalls in FY 2012. While some sources predict that half of the states will have large gaps in FY 2013, other studies project that all fifty states will face continuing budget deficits by that date. And the fifty states already face a daunting $300 billion budget gap!

Consider that the Obama Administration's stimulus package provided $200 billion to state and local governments over a three-year fiscal period 2010-2012. And note that more that 55 percent of that bailout was spent in the first year, with 33 percent in FY 2011, leaving just 12 percent for FY 2012. Even with the August 2010 $26 billion "son of stimulus" additional bailout funds for Medicaid and K-12 teaching positions, the ultimate question still has to be faced: What happens to state and local governments when that cash from the Big Daddy Beltway ends?

Many academic leaders plan to lobby their way back to prosperity. Some are conducting studies to "document their contributions to the state" assuming that will lead to new revenue. Some believe the last three years are "just a cyclical thing". And some misguidedly believe that more money will be forthcoming because "they deserve it." But as Thomas Donlan, *Barron's* editorial page editor, correctly observes, "Begging for money from insolvent state government is impractical." And Anthony Caravale of the University of Georgia agrees, noting that states will not have serious new money until at least 2015. (And even then they will have K-12 education, welfare, prisons and numerous other hands out.) As 2010 ended, numerous national reports including the National Conference of State Legislatures and the American Association of State Colleges and Universities confirmed the unrelenting financial squeeze confronting higher education. So if higher education is looking for new megabucks from the state, that cookie jar is empty and likely will remain so for years.

What about the federal government? Already the public research universities have switched their focus to the US Treasury, reasoning that the government came through with substantial stimulus funds and that transfusion curtailed some of the bloodletting that would have taken place otherwise. But most of that money will have been spent by the end of FY 2012, and the federal government has massive debt problems of its own, a legislative climate that is hardly conducive to more bailouts, and an unsustainable mountain of entitlements.

The United States spent $2 trillion on health care in 2009, an amount larger than the GDP of Russia, France and Brazil combined. The increasing cost of Medicare (which covers 45 million Americans) and Medicaid (which covers 30 million more) is weighing heavily on the Beltway. Another major area of entitlement is Social Security, which is on the road to insolvency by 2037 in a best-case scenario. In 1960 there were five workers to support each retiree; 3.2 in 2008; and by 2030 there will be just 2.2. Worse, as Rudolph Penne of the Urban Institute says, we continually magnify our problem by "ever increasing the benefits." A rash of early retirements by people who have given up looking for work, will add to the system an even greater burden than was anticipated prior to the recent economic crisis.

During the Great Recession, the federal government extended regular state unemployment benefits six times. After the typical twenty-six weeks of state funding, the federal government added twenty weeks, then as the recession continued it added fourteen, thirteen, and six weeks until finally in December of 2010, it added thirteen *months* more! In total, an unemployed worker can now receive up to *three years* of unemployment as part of the Bush tax-cut extension (the "third stimulus package" costing $858 billion). That amount eclipsed the $814 stimulus package of 2009.

The new Congress, however, faces a massive $13 trillion debt—more than $40,000 for every man, woman and child living in America! We have been kicking the can so far down the road that as Gene Sperling so aptly sums it up, we have made "unsustainable promises." Worse, we are so deeply hemmed in by these promises that as early as FY 2009 "every single dollar of revenue was committed before Congress voted on any new spending program." Jeffrey Sachs expands on that dire portrait noting that if all the anticipated federal revenue would pay for just four major programs: health care, social security, military spending and debt payment. Everything else is being paid for on borrowed money! Things like funds for state and local governments, homeland security, and outlays for higher education–all done by borrowing. The federal government may be able to print money, but there is a price to be paid in terms of inflation, national security and ever greater encumbrances on our younger generations who are going to have to pay the piper.

Currently Congress spends $3 for every $2 it takes in. Federal debt will increase $1.6 trillion in FY 2011 alone–an amount that incidentally is higher than our national budget of fifteen years ago. Under current spending plans, the debt will grow by an additional $4.5 trillion by 2015. And Fareed Zakaria warns that "Over the next seventy-five years, benefits under entitlement programs will exceed government revenue by $40 trillion. The federal budget deficit, if unattended, will reach 24 percent of the GNP by 2040."

Given such dire fiscal realities and projections, even Secretary of Education Arne Duncan admits that the federal government can do only so much for postsecondary education. "If at the end of the day, they think they are going to be able to avoid making hard decisions," he said in December 2009, "that is unrealistic." Higher education is no longer going to be able to rely on Washington, DC bailouts. That message came as clear as a bell when Congress stunned the academic world–and the nation–by curtailing earmarks for FY 2011. Higher education lost $1.5 billion it had counted on receiving. More federal money? As a typical Texan might observe, "That dog won't hunt!"

The White House has directed federal agencies to reduce their budgets by 5 percent and some of the possible savings in the Department of Education are 150 "program redundancies" within the department, according to Peter Orszag the president's former budget director. So, without a doubt, higher education is not going to emerge from the Great Recession and simply return to "the thrilling days of yesteryear." That conclusion is backed with the strong credentials of David Gergen, editor-at-large for *US News & World Report* when he warned "Universities are facing a New Normal."

We couldn't agree more.

The fable, *Our Iceberg Is Melting,* by John Kotter of the Harvard Business School, contains a pointed message for tertiary education. The story tells of a group of empire penguins. One discovers that the iceberg they have called home for as far back as they can remember is melting. The leaders of the community are skeptical and resistant–exchanges that resonate as extremely familiar–before being convinced that change is inevitable. The question then becomes, "What are they going to do about it?" We wouldn't want to tip the ending but they do arrive at a solution that demands change. The lesson for higher education is: "PSSST. . .Your iceberg really *is* melting!"

While we still have you "on ice," let's underline a lesson from hockey great Wayne Gretzky. When asked why he was such a great player, he said, "Most players skate to where the puck is. I skate to where it is going to be." Higher education must lace up its skates and go *there* as well.

Although the scope is larger and the stakes higher than in my Citrus College computer class, the lesson is the same: We must delete or modify that which is no longer needed or relevant and concentrate on delivering what students, employers and our nation needs.

Cosmetic change isn't going to cut it. We need a fundamental makeover, a systematic and structural explosion!

Chapter VI

# GENERATIONAL BARBELLS

"The incomes of the young and middle-aged
have fallen off the cliff since 2000."
Dennis Cauchon
*USA Today*

When my daughter Shelby graduated from San Diego State University, we took a father-daughter weekend trip to New York City. We were typical tourists. We visited the Empire State Building, the United Nations, Radio City Music Hall, the Statue of Liberty, Macy's department store (as a family we watched *Miracle on 34th Street* every Christmas), Sardi's, and saw a Broadway revival of *The Graduate*. That was where *it* happened! Standing across the street from the theater I was gazing at a large billboard of Kathleen Turner. I remarked, "Wasn't it great to see someone in person whom you had seen on the silver screen?" Shelby readily nodded in agreement. She, however, was looking at the other billboard featuring Jason Biggs.

We were looking at the actors from the perspective of two different generations.

According to Neil Howe and William Strauss, there have been nineteen identifiable generations since the Mayflower landed in 1620. Historians clump groups of people together based upon uncommon occurrences that tend to shape a certain period of time. They tend to prefer ten-, fifteen-, or even twenty-year blocks themed around events such as Pearl Harbor, the fall of the Berlin Wall, or the terrorist New York City attack of 9/11. These seminal events are marked in our cultural common memory and are events that each generation will never forget. They form our attitudes. They forge a common bond. They affect our behaviors. They focus our actions.

When I was a child of five, I remember attaching my roller skates to my shoes, wearing a sailor's hat, blowing a whistle, and waving a small American flag as a part of a massive celebration. Although a full participant in the festivities, I did not know until I was a bit older that the event was the end of World War II.

I remember my mom taking margarine from the ice box, adding a small packet of yellow coloring, and squeezing it like grease in her hands to make it look more like butter. And I have a vague recollection of something called "rationing," but it would not be until I was forty that the term would be fully understood by "the younger generation." In 1973 for the first time for many, we saw long lines at gasoline stations and limits on how much fuel was available during the Oil Embargo.

On November 22, 1963, I was a graduate student at Purdue University. Early that morning I was walking through the Memorial Union on my way to Heavilon Hall when I noticed something unusual: A large number of students were gathered around the television set in one of the large areas off the corridor. I paused to see what might be focusing everyone's attention and saw Walter Cronkite repeating that the President of the United States of America had been shot in Dallas. The news was jolting. In stunned disbelief, I sat down on a sofa between two students that I did not know waiting to hear more.

What was happening was happening to all of us. We were each internalizing it. Virtually no one left the room for the next few hours and the growing crowd stood silent. It wasn't long until the nation learned that

President John F. Kennedy had died. Over the next few days a morbid pall consumed the campus, the state and the nation. Only after the nationally televised funeral did we start to return to our daily routines.

That tragedy will forever be one of my most vivid memories. It made me more than a graduate student. It was perhaps one of the motivating factors that caused me to seek and be elected to the Michigan Legislature in 1972. But that historic event did not happen to just *one* generation; it happened to multiple generations, as did World War I, World War II, the Great Depression, the New Deal, the New Frontier, 9/11, and the Great Recession of 2007-2010.

There have been numerous books and articles written on the subject of generational distinctions. If you take time to carefully review a number of them, you will discover four things..

First, the generational labels are inconsistent. Limiting ourselves to the six generations alive today, the labels change from "GI" to "Traditionalists" for those born before 1925; the "Silent Generation," "Depressionists," or "Radio Babies" for those born before World War II; "Boomers" or "Baby Boomers" for those born between the early 1940s and mid 1960s; "Generation X" for those from the latter 1960s to the late 1970s; "Generation Y" or "Millennials for those born between the late 1970s and late 1990s; and "Post-Millennials" or "iGen" for those born in the last ten-to-fifteen years. Second, the dates defining a particular generation vary (starting and ending) from source to source.

Third, the number of people who fall into a particular generation can differ by several million. Finally, many of the distinctions made seem forced, artificial, or directed at marketing.

Without getting too specific about labels, starting and ending dates, and reasons for separation, let's retreat to Neil Howe and William Strauss for some sage advice. They tell us that "people do not belong to their age brackets." Each person is the sum of individual experiences that cut across generational bracketing.

During the mid-1990s when I was a member of the Texas Federal Reserve Board, we made continual recommendations not to change the discount rate. The economy was constantly robust and the parade of expert economists seemed to believe that the nation had evolved to such an innovative level that the economy would continue to expand. Therefore, prospects for the future were bright. That seemed to be good advice until we "hit the economic wall." Then, thud!

Quickly and alarmingly, starting with Goldman Sachs, the cloth on the national economic cloak started to unravel. Or as Warren Buffet might say, "It is hard to tell who is swimming without a bathing suit until the tide goes out." Well, for the USA (and much of the world) the tide went out in 2007, and the inadequacies of our economic swimwear exposed our posteriors. The resulting economic meltdown has affected all six living generations. How? In terms of competition for resources. If we view the six generations as race horses, they all can't "win," "place" or "show"! Only one will receive the top purse. Two will receive sizable but lesser rewards. Three generations will finish out of the money.

Before the Great Recession, the economy looked so robust that issues of federal, state and local debt–and unsustainable promises–were far beneath the surface. Everyone knew that Social Security, Medicare and Medicaid were in some trouble, but that issue was hazily out there somewhere in the future. The Great Recession provided a starkly unanticipated realization of the clear and present danger. And, although all six living generations were, are and will be affected, the significance of the problem might best be viewed in terms of a barbell with two large weights (in people) on each end of 1955.

According to census data reported by Dennis Cauchon, there is "a dividing line between those getting richer or poorer and the fault line is 1955. "If you were born before that you're part of a generation enjoying a four-decade run of historic income growth," he says, and "every generation after that is now sinking economically." And William Frey of the Brookings Institution concurs saying that the split between the aging and the young will result in a "huge cleavage." That gap grew wider during the recession.

Anya Kamenetz, in *Generation Debt*, puts the barbell illustration to pen. Her contention is that the younger generations have been sold out and that the older generations have been greedy. In 2010, the average college graduate had loan debt totaling $23,000, despite the fact that 49 percent of full-time college students had full- or part-time jobs. Add to her concerns that unemployment runs rampant at 15 percent for those ages twenty to twenty-four. Indeed the 2010 labor force was composed of an estimated 28 million people age fifty-five or older and just 17 million age sixteen-to-twenty-four. A snapshot of Generation Y (late teens and twenty-somethings) is provided by Christine Dugas in *USA Today*: "Stagnant wages, job insecurity, the decline in employer-sponsored health insurance and retirement benefits, the rapid increase in basic expenses, and soaring debt and minimal savings have jeopardized the economic security of the entire generation."

Moving up to Generation X (roughly those age twenty-nine to forty-five), there is far less job security. In 1980, more than 60 percent of workers received a traditional defined pension, but by the time Generation X joined the workforce that number had reversed itself. The old corporate safety net had been replaced with voluntary 401(k) plans. Dugas' case is strong and her concerns far transcend student debt, employment opportunities and pensions.

Think about it. Currently 50 million seniors collect Social Security payments that average $14,000 a year. No wonder, then, that in 2010, trust-fund trustees projected that the "break-even date" (when pay-outs will exceed the payroll tax that funds the program) will hit in 2016. Sure the program has a $2.4 trillion trust fund, but that fund, under present conditions, will be exhausted by 2037. Add to that the fact that 46 million people over the age of sixty-five received more than $500 billion in benefits in 2009, and that exhaustion date becomes 2029.

Because neither political party will approach this with a ten-foot pole, President Obama appointed a bipartisan commission to render a Social Security solution. The last such commission produced adjustments in 1983 when Congress raised the full-benefit age of retirement from sixty-five to sixty-seven. But being ever sensitive to the need to get re-elected they phased in the two-year age increase over forty years! (Talk about too little, too late.) This time around, the Federal Budget Reduction Commission made bold recommendations toward cutting $4 trillion during the next decade. Virtually no sacred cows were kept off the table. The road map leading toward financial stability is clear, but the political reality is that the recommendations are composed of one political hot potato after another. Social Security is only one of the big three entitlements; Medicare and Medicaid are in a similar place. Then add the $700 billion Bush bailout of the banking system, the Obama $787 billion economic stimulus package and the cost of the new health-care program to the younger generation's tab and the total US debt comes to $13 trillion and growing. And what about paying the bill?

Basically the issues are the same for higher education. We have been living beyond our means and need to face up to reality. The question is, will we?

On the other end of the demographic barbell sit 150 million people who have worked throughout their careers to secure their piece of the "good-life" pie. They were home owners, had modest savings, and had defined company pensions and health benefits; a large number had invested in stocks. Retired or nearing retirement, they were looking forward to retirement and a few–maybe several–golden years. When the stock market bottomed out in the spring of 2009, stocks fell to their 2003 level and home values plunged more than 40 percent below their 2006 peak, the Boomers' sense of security was badly shaken. The Employee Benefit Research Institute estimates that, almost half of the Baby boomers ages fifty-six to sixty-two may not have enough savings for even basic expenses. At the same time, many retired or near-retirement Americans are providing financial help to their children and grandchildren—not to mention their elderly parents. Before the Great Recession, theirs was the generation brimming with confidence. Now they worry that they will not have enough to get by.

One fallout has been significant growth in multigenerational housing. During the Great Recession one in every ten young adults (eighteen to thirty-four) moved back in with their parents. In 2008 some 50 million Americans lived in a household of two adult generations, a number nearly double what it was twenty years earlier. A recent AARP survey found that almost 7 million US households are made up of three generations or more, a figure one-third larger than a decade earlier. Both builders and real estate agents believe these trends will continue. Even single-generation families are seeking smaller homes, and the trend of first marriage at a later date has been exacerbated. By 2008, 28 percent of women over sixteen and 35 percent of the men had never married.

The three-pronged thrift lesson deeply embedded into the psyche of those who lived through the Great Depression was: avoid debt, pay in cash and save. That value habit lasted for four decades, but began to wane at about 14 percent of income in 1975. By 1985, the rate of savings approached zero and Americans were living beyond their means. Then in 2008, household income took its largest drop since the government started collecting that information sixty years ago, falling nearly 4 percent. The dollar drop was steep enough to wipe out a decade of gains is just one year and jobs were so difficult to come by that 2.6 million workers selected Social Security in 2009.

Add to this scenario the "bonus years" worry. Today, people over sixty-five can expect to live into their eighties. They worry that they may not have the wherewithal to afford it. The other end of the barbell has grown nervous over the growing cost. They worry that within the next forty years there may be as many as 800,000 Americans who live to become centennials. Both ends of the barbell realize the great cost that goes with longer life expectancies.

### Who will pay?

One bright note for both ends of the barbell is the "encore career" movement. With better health and longer years to live, many older workers are seeking a second or even third career. When senior executives were asked in June of 2008 if their company would hire a qualified seventy-two-year-old CEO, almost half said they would. This desire to keep working after traditional retirement age, accounts for the fact that 25 percent of "kids" between sixty-five and seventy-four are in the workforce. Marc Freedman, in his 2007 book *Encore*, labels this movement "one of the most profound social trends of our century." He traces the changing paradigm as "freedom *from* work, to freedom *to* work," noting that large numbers of older Americans are "searching for a calling, purpose, fulfillment and meaning." That bodes well for both ends of the barbell, since 20 percent of our population will be sixty-five or older by 2030.

In May 2010, The Robert Half Company surveyed three generations (generations Y and X, and baby boomers) ranging from ages twenty-one to sixty-four, asking: "Has the Great Recession changed the perceptions of multiple generations about the workplace?" They discovered that what the three generations wanted was really not so different. Compensation, benefits and stability were the top three when considering employment. All three generations prized health care and time off. Almost half planned to work beyond age sixty-five.

And, although our population will grow from 300 million to 400 million by 2050, there is more good news. Our country is better off in "barbell" terms than most of the rest of the world. Our fertility rate is much higher than that of China, Japan, Russia, South Korea and Eastern Europe, and our population between the ages of fifteen and sixty-four will grow by 40 percent during those same years. Meanwhile, our elder side of the barbell (sixty-five and older) will grown 100 percent between now and 2040, while the rate of elder growth for the same population segment in Egypt, Malaysia, India, Columbia and Singapore will double or triple ours.

Although six generational horses are approaching the gate, the great race will focus on the two favorites: the 78 million baby boomers and the 80 million millennials.

The competition is going to be brutal!

Chapter VII

# LESSONS FROM "OVER THERE"

"Education is an economic issue
when we know beyond a shadow of a doubt
that countries which out-educate us today
will out-compete us tomorrow."
Barack Obama

It happens every spring. What sports announcer Dick Vitale calls, "Bas-ket-ball, Ba-by!" Sixty-four college basketball teams are invited to the national tournament to decide which is number one! Over a three-week elimination schedule, the men's and women's brackets go from sixty-four to thirty-two, to the sweet sixteen, the elite eight, the final four, and the championship game ultimately determining who has the right to be known as the best university basketball team in the nation!

The quest for being first is ubiquitous.

College football and baseball and other sports have a national playoff schedule to compete for bragging rights. So do the pros. Whether for hockey's Stanley Cup or football's Super Bowl, the quest to be number one is ever present. Baseball even has the audacity to declare its number one as the "World Series Champion," even though only two nations compete.

This desire to be number one permeates business, higher education, and virtually everything else in our culture. Americans are obsessed with the thought. We have got to be at the top of the ladder–or at least believe we are. And for the past century we have been first in almost every category. But the world has been and is changing, and some of the paradigm shift in numbers may be surprising but *not* delightful.

While an undergraduate student at Detroit's Wayne State University, it was my great fortune to study debate with perhaps the best coach in America, George "Zig" Ziegelmueller. Zig was bright and articulate. He could explain complex thoughts in a short sentence. During one class period he was explaining "sign reasoning"–a term that made little sense to me at the time. His example was, "If the lights are on, there is a good chance someone was home." Being a challenging student I responded, "We leave some lights on when we are not home." Zig explained that when you are trying to reach a conclusion, you could read a series of signs that would move you toward certainty. For example, if several lights are on, if the television is on, or if you should hear a door open or close. It is the series of signs, one on top of the other that will eventually lead to a well-based conclusion.

That lecture has stayed with me all these years, and I want to relate a series of signs that, in compilation, will lead to a warranted conclusion: American higher education is in a world of hurt; the pain is increasing in intensity; and it is high time for our hundred-year-old paradigm to change.

Let's start with something basic. Do you have any idea where Americans stand in the world? I mean physically.

- According to John Komolos of the University of Munich, American men check in at ninth tallest in the world and our women rank at fifteenth. The tallest people in the world are the Dutch, followed by the Danes.
- The world's tallest building now belongs to the United Arab Emirates. Compared to the USA's 1,729 foot Willis Tower in

Chicago, the Burj Dubai soars 900 yards into the sky–the length of nine football fields!

- In the 2010 Winter Olympics, although our media tended to report total medals won, we ranked third–behind Canada and Germany–in gold medals.
- The world's largest shopping mall is in Beijing.
- Largest casino? Macao.
- Fifteen nations have better cell phone service.
- The global leader in higher education completion rates for young adults is Canada.

In terms of world economic competitiveness, the findings in the World Economic Forum's 2009-2010 Global Competitiveness Report are downright alarming. The report has been providing benchmarking tools for the past 30 years. In 2005 the forum developed and began using a Global Competitive Index (GCI) based upon "twelve pillars of competitiveness": institutions, infrastructure, macroeconomic stability, health and primary education, higher education and training, goods-market efficiency, labor-market efficiency, financial market sophistication, technological readiness, market size, business sophistication, and innovation. Reporting both survey and hard data, the comprehensive written and tabled findings cover 133 countries, are translated into twenty languages, and have become a widely accepted and respected assessment of national competitiveness. Among the findings in the most recent report:

Switzerland has replaced the USA as the world's most competitive economy.

We rank forty-third in trust of our politicians, thirty-first in transparency of government policymaking, twenty-first in reliability of police service, twenty-second in ethical behavior of firms, and thirty-ninth in strength of auditing and reporting standards.

In terms of overall quality of infrastructure, we rank fourteenth. Our national savings rate ranks 109, government budget balance is 122, inflation is ranked twentieth, interest rate spread is number twelve, governmental debt is 114, life expectancy thirtieth, and infant mortality rate thirty-eighth.

Our K-12 educational rankings are not a reason for joy. Our primary school enrollment of 92.4 percent places us at seventy-seventh, and our placement for secondary enrollment forty-third.

All of this is leads up to the fact that even though our higher education officials constantly pronounce America's system of higher education as "the best in the world," mounting evidence suggests otherwise. At the very least, we are in danger of losing that status in the near future.

In terms of enrollment at the college or advanced-education level, the World Economic Forum ranks us as sixth, coming in behind Korea, Finland, Greece, Slovenia and Taiwan. The Organization for Economic Co-operation and Development (OECD), a Paris based organization with a thirty-democracy membership, tells us that while we are still the most highly educated nation in the world (with 39 percent of Americans aged twenty-five to sixty-four holding an associate degree or higher), that overall attainment rate can be deceiving.

The college completion rate for younger Americans (ages twenty-five to thirty-four) has shown virtually no gain for the past thirty years. In order for us to reach President Obama's goal of having the highest rate of college graduates in the world by 2020, we would have to increase the attainment rate from the current 40 percent to 60 percent for young Americans–an increase of 10 million two- and four-year degrees by 2020. Among the thirty-six developed nations of the world, we rank twelfth in attainment for this age group, and America's college drop-our (or stopout) rate has become one of our major national concerns. While 64 percent of young Americans entered college in 2005, only 57 percent graduated in six years. That "survival rate" puts us last on the OEDC list, tied with New Zealand.

While the US has been treading water, a few nations are stepping back in terms of higher education support (Britain, Italy, Ireland and Greece) but other countries have mightily increased their stroke and their speed is accelerating. Consider that in 2007 we ranked tenth in access, down from number seven the year before–a decline of three places in just one year.

We rank near the bottom in the proportion of twenty-five year-olds who have earned degrees in natural science or engineering when compared with European and Asian nations. No doubt, much of the world is playing leap-frog in terms of younger Americans with these critical skills.

If you haven't done so yet, we would highly recommend reading Fareed Zakaria's *The Post-American World*, even if you find the title off-putting. What he describes runs counter to our typical isolationist view that what goes on in the rest of the world (unless it's a war) is of little interest to us. Zakaria paints a portrait of "the rise of the rest" while we are painting by the same tired old numbers. He labels the economic betterment of numerous countries as the "great story of our time." That deliberate message is articulated from a slightly different viewpoint in Thomas Friedman's *The World is Flat*–and he, too, is right.

Between 2000 and 2006, other national growth rates were impressive: New Zealand, 700 percent; The Netherlands, 160 percent; Japan, 95 percent; and Sweden, 60 percent. But this "rise of the rest" has made little impression on the American mind. The massive advancement has not been noticed, acknowledged, or understood in the USA. The twin forces of globalization and nationalism are feeding upon new-found economic strength in China, India, Brazil and many other nations, and these forces are reshaping political power, national pride, national will, and national aspirations.

After America won the Cold War, our way of life became the world model for success. We were envied for our standard of living, mimicked in our cultural tastes, and carbon copied in numerous social ways. Our economic model became the global "gold standard." Although that happened selectively and slowly at first, the pace for other nations and regions to move toward our standard has quickened. Over the past decade or more, the pace has resembled a sticking Toyota accelerator.

The world's population will reach 7 billion in 2011. Let's take a look at what this means for American higher education.

China, with its 1.3 billion people, has been "large but poor" for most of its history. But thirty years ago, a dramatic transformation started. Regardless of the political ideology, China embraced modernization and economic development with both hands. As a result, China has courted double-digit economic growth for three decades. By 2010, according to the Paris-based International Energy Agency, China has become the world leader in energy consumption. That milestone was reached five years ahead of schedule and underlines the dramatic progress from a nation of rural farmers riding bicycles into a developing superpower. During the same year China replaced Japan as the second largest economy in the world–Japan had held that distinction for the past three decades. That change has been labeled by economist Jeffrey Sachs as the "most successful development story in the world." And the World Bank speculates that China might surpass the US as the world's largest economy as early as 2020.

That enormous economic growth (12 percent in the first quarter of 2010) sparked rapid improvement in higher education there in the 1980s. With Projects 985 and 211 backed by central government funding, China has vigorously (to the tune of $3 billion) pursued its goal of building twenty globally acknowledged universities. Today, two Chinese universities (Peking and Tsinghua) already sit among the top 100 and a handful of others have become internationally competitive. China's Ministry of Education only last October formed a C9 Conference of nine elite universities self-described as "China's Ivy League." China has also created academies of science institutes throughout the country.

Today China boasts a higher literacy rate than ours (90 percent vs. 86 percent). There are more English-speaking Chinese than our entire 305 million population, and English is one of the three compulsory subjects taught in their grade schools. Being a native of Detroit, it did not escape my attention that in 2005 China became the largest automobile market in the world. China also has more Starbucks! Even if you are looking for a literal "apples to apples" comparison, China produces nearly 60 billion pounds; the USA produces one-sixth of that.

In the past two decades, university enrollment of traditional age Chinese students has zoomed from 3 percent to 23 percent. China already has the largest higher educational system on the globe and they aim to double participation rates in the near future. China has a sense of destiny and higher education is a vital link in that interlocking chain.

India, with its 1.1 billion current population is projected to become the most populous nation on the globe by 2020. Since 1997, their gross domestic product (GDP) has grown by an average of 7 percent annually. Some 13 million students now attend college in India and Education Minister Kapil Sibal announced last year his desire to have 30 percent of the country's students go on to college–a staggering number given the 220 million students in the country's primary and secondary schools. An ambitious new Right to Education Act takes effect there this spring.

The European Higher Education Area (EHEA) was initiated in Bologna, Italy in 1999 when twenty-one nations signed a declaration with several objectives: to adopt a system of comparable degrees; to establish a system of credits; to promote mobility for students and faculty; to enhance quality assurance; and to foster European interests in higher education. In essence, by establishing a geographic block that would define the EHEA, the objective was to become the world's leading knowledge-economy block.

Over the next few years, Ministerial Conferences held in Prague (2001), Berlin (2003), Bergen (2005), London (2007), and Leuaven/Louvain-la-Neuve (2009), will be expanded by the EHEA to forty-six countries. This behemoth, multinational higher education entity did not gain life via an intergovernmental treaty. Nothing was legally binding–each nation could participate in EHEA initiatives on an *a la carte* basis. But as the Bologna compact celebrated its tenth anniversary in 2010, the international peer pressure had yielded great substance; so much so, that articles and books about what America can learn from the process have started to appear in the last few months.

The Bologna Process created a sense of urgency–a coordinated commitment to reforms in higher learning and a two-year check-off master list to measure output. Among EHEA's handiwork (although not uniformly applied) is a full focus on a three-year bachelor degree. As a result of their leadership in that area, several colleges in the USA are now beginning to offer three-year degrees and more will do so (if they follow our advice in Chapter XII). EHEA has now set goals for 2020.

Other nations that had typically followed America's lead are starting to form areas or blocks of their own. Don Olcott, Chief Executive Officer of the Observatory of Borderless Higher Education, refers to this happening as the "new global regionalism." He asks, "Are we really naïve enough to think that China, India, Malaysia, South Korea, the Gulf States, and others do not want to build long-term, high-quality, sustainable university systems in their countries and regions to serve their students? It would not be the first time, or probably the last, that Western countries have completely misread global developments."

John Douglass of the Center for Studies in Higher Education at UC Berkley notes that, while the US pioneered the move to mass higher education, it "seems to have stopped innovating and could be losing its first-mover advantage." He labels our national completion numbers "torpid," cautioning that "while the US largely treads water in the race for human capital. . .other nations are making major progress, largely focused on expanding tertiary access, achieving more robust graduation rates, and competing more effectively for talent." He grades us as "mediocre" in getting students into college and "poor" at degree completion.

That could be a bit of an understatement.

Singling out California, he notes that access to higher education for traditional age students declined significantly between 1970 (55 percent) and 2000 (48 percent). In contrast, in England higher education enrollment has grown by 30 percent and by 72 percent in France over the past twenty years. In fact, OECD reports that many nations are currently matching or exceeding US college completion rates. (Among OECD nations we rank sixteenth.) Douglass concludes that "perhaps the world economy and priorities of competitor nations have permanently eroded America's once-distinct higher education advantage." He suggests that "America should look across the oceans to other continents for ideas, inspiration, and a pragmatic sense of the globalizing and increasingly competitive world."

For example, in the past twenty years Australia made three significant strategic policy decisions in higher education that are now paying big dividends. First, they radically shifted from a no-tuition policy to a Higher Education Contribution System (HECS). Whereas the old system was government *funded*, the new system is government *subsidized*. Basically, the government makes loans to students according to their need, and graduates repay via the income tax, after annual income reaches a certain level. Second, the sixty-five "Down Under" universities and colleges of advanced education were collapsed into half that number for greater efficiencies. Third, the commonwealth strongly encouraged institutions to generate some of their own funds, and considerable success has been achieved in attracting international students, bringing their total up to 25 percent of overall enrollment.

Germany, via its Excellence Initiative, has invested $2.8 billion on research and higher education in the past five years and has established a handful of new German Centers for Research and Innovation in Moscow, New Delhi, Tokyo, Brazil and the US. Each center is provided with $4 million from the education ministry. Both investments speak to that nation's increasing reputation for research.

Sweden provides its 350,000 students with a full government subsidy and there is currently no tuition cost. In fall 2010, however, they will start charging tuition to new international students who are not from the European Union, the European Economic Area, or native to Sweden. (The number of such foreigners has grown to more than 28,000 students.) Sweden's Minister of Higher Education Tobias Krantz notes that higher education is a global market and "free" tuition does not target the best or most desirable internationals. Institutions will be allowed to establish their own tuition rate, but the clear goal is full-cost recovery.

Advancement by "the others" in terms of higher education goes on: Singapore is planning for its fourth new public university; South Korea is spending billions designing high-power research laboratories; and Taiwan has set its sights on attracting the lucrative international student market.

All of Asia is on the move, and the Great Recession of the past two years could expedite their advantage. For example, China maintained higher learning effort and spending momentum in 2010, while South Korea (and Brazil) actually dug deeper and supplied more funding during the two-year recession.

Is American higher education STILL the best in the world? According to the QS World University Rankings of 2010, seven of the world's top universities were not in the USA. In fact, half of the top thirty and sixty-nine of the top hundred were "over there."

Another sign for concern is the number of nations that are targeting the international student market which has historically favored the US and Great Britain. Why is this important? Consider three points.

First, with the economic "rise of the others," comes a gain in perceived quality and prestige. The result is that the US is no longer *seen* as the singular or ultimate place to study.

Second, global higher education is a growing market according to the OECD. Postsecondary students studying in other than their native countries now tally 3 million, and that number will continue to climb. One estimate is 8 million by 2025.

Third, the international student market is lucrative. In the US foreign students bring in almost $16 billion yearly in tuition and related revenue. France ranks fourth in attracting international students behind the US, the U.K. and Germany, and a full one-third of the graduate students in France are internationals. And the *Economist* ranks Canada, the Netherlands, Singapore, Malaysia and Japan as new "serious competitors."

Australia for more than a decade also has been hard at work attracting international students. Since forming the Australian Educational International, a staffed governmental agency, there has been a 75 percent growth (between 2000 and 2006) and this market now brings in $12 billion annually in US dollars.

Yet another competition factor is being able to keep international students here after they've completed their education. That's important for several reasons, such as economic development beyond tuition and living expenses. Large numbers of international students make up our science, math and engineering graduates, and have skills that can benefit our growth. Truth be told, though, many of these international graduates can now find more lucrative jobs and opportunities in their native countries.

So what lessons can we learn from "over there?" Several. First, the "rise of the others" *is* the great story of our time. Although the world is not flat, it is becoming flatter. And with the rise in economic fortunes comes new vitality and vision. Second, the American desire to be number one is not unique to us as a people. As Bill Gates tells us, "China, India and the others are not racing us to the bottom–they are racing us to the top." Third, revisiting "sign reasoning" (in Professor Zig fashion), a clear conclusion is warranted: both developed and developing nations, all over the globe are increasing their horsepower, revving up their engines and preparing to eclipse the mile-markers on the higher education highway.

Over the next decade that pathway will heat up like Atlanta asphalt in mid-August!

Chapter XIII

# THE CALIFORNIA BELLWETHER

"A convergence of other pressures and the American economy
have eroded the ability of states to rebuild
their financial support for higher education."
Paul Lingenfelter
President, State Higher Education Executive Officers


What happens in Vegas may stay in Vegas, but what happens in California does not!

With its nearly 40 million people (one out of every eight people in this country) the Golden State would be the world's ninth largest economy if it were a separate nation. California has been a trendsetter for as long as it has been a state. Nationally, it is regarded as a leading liberal state, but a pundit once quipped that "it occasionally comes to its senses."

The source of one-quarter of the patents filed annually in the USA, most Americans would acknowledge California as a trendsetter in styles and fads, and on the cutting edge when it comes to new ways of thinking. Why should it be any different in terms of the Great Recession? According to recent studies, California was hit harder than any other state in the nation. In November 2009, the Pew Center on the States reported that California "was in a league of its own" in terms of recession impact. The state was so far out in front, in fact, that the organization used it as a reference point to compare the relative position of all fifty states. The Pew study rated the states on a six-factor scale: revenue, budget gap, unemployment, foreclosures, state fiscal management, and the requirement of a "super majority" (two-thirds vote of the state legislature) to raise taxes and ratify budgets. On a scale of one (best) to thirty (worst) California garnered the lone "thirty" distinction.

And in December 2009, the National Association of State Budget Officers confirmed California as holding the worst state position. Why? Three primary reasons were cited.

First, as then-Governor Arnold Schwarzenegger pointed out in his 2010 State of the State address, "Our economy is twenty-first century and our tax system is twentieth century." In FY 2009, California's economy slid by 3 percent while state revenues declined by more than 20 percent. Take the state's personal income tax, for example: A mere 1 percent of the state's population (144,000 of 38 million residents) pays almost 50 percent of the tax. Property taxes fell statewide for the first time since 1933 (when the California Board of Equalization began keeping annual tabulations) a drop in assessed valuations of $107 billion. Meanwhile at midyear 2010, 12.5 percent of the population was unemployed. California now also ranks dead last in state bond ratings, meaning more interest has to be paid when borrowing.

Second, the legislative and executive leadership of the state relied on smoke and mirrors in passing recent budgets. Even after lollygagging and eventually maneuvering around its $27 billion FY 2010 shortfall with a concoction of IOU's, short-term taxes, furloughs for state workers, federal stimulus money and extensive borrowing, cuts of more than $7 billion had to be made by June 30, 2010 to balance the budget. A November 2009 report by the Legislative Analyst's office anticipated a deficit of $14 billion for FY 2011; by summer the number had swollen to $19 billion.

Although almost everyone inside and even outside of California has internalized the $19 billion budget shortfall put out by the Schwarzenegger Administration, it proved to be a figure long on mendacity. The governor's budget assumed a phantom $6.9 billion would be coming from the Beltway, millions would be rolling in from off-shore drilling that has yet to be authorized, the ability to raid local governmental coffers (being fought with lawsuits), and numerous other "shell games." By Labor Day 2010, with no final resolution of the state budget, Governor Schwarzenegger ordered 144,000 state workers to take three unpaid furloughs each month and the Golden State anticipated paying its bills with IOU's for the third time in its history. Shock and awe gave way to slash and burn. The deficit now projected through FY 2012 is $27 billion.

An old adage advises, "When you're in a hole, stop digging," but Sacramento may not have that option. California, until recently, was the only state in the nation that required a super-majority two-thirds vote to pass both a state tax increase and the state budget. (An initiative passed in November 2010 now allows for the state budget to be passed by a simple majority). Looking out across the next five years a Legislative Analyst's Office report makes some key assumptions: MediCal funding would rise by more than $7 billion and prison spending would go up by $2 billion, and there would be no pay increases or cost-of-living adjustments for state workers. Community colleges would see a drop in funding and both the California State University and University of California systems would receive zero new funds.

Third, California (more than any other state) has straight-jacketed itself by referendums passed by the voters. Oftentimes these initiatives are spearheaded by out-of-state economic or political interests. The greatest fault-line in the Golden State may not be the San Andreas; it might well be the state's reefer-madness referendum habit. In the spring of 2010, fifty-nine petitions were being circulated for the November election. And both the legislative leaders and the people themselves can claim equal credit.

This last point is crucial, because although nearly half the states allow a ballot-initiative process for statutory or constitutional change, California is unique, extreme and even bizarre when it comes to initiatives. Consider that the US Constitution has been amended only seventeen times since it was adopted in 1788, while the California Constitution has been amended more than 500 times since 1879. The result is a crazy quilt of special-interest measures. With only 433,000 signatures you can have chance to change a law and with just 700,000 petition signers you get an opportunity to change the state constitution. That's almost a slam dunk for deep-pocket special interest groups who simply hire signature gatherers to get the job done–some firms actually guarantee petition success. Also the California Constitution can be amended by a simple majority of votes cast.

The granddaddy all initiatives was Proposition 13, passed on June 6, 1978 by a super-majority of voters. That historic measure made three bedrock decisions: first, property taxes were reduced by 57 percent and limited to 1 percent of full cash value; second, property-tax increases would be a maximum of 2 percent per year; third, any increase in taxes would take a two-thirds vote of the electorate or the state legislature. Those 389 words were inserted into the constitution and three decades later the full extent of the harm is clearly visible. Before Prop 13 more than half of school budgets came from local property taxes, today that number is approximately 20 percent. Over the years a complex formula was developed as a result of a series of laws and ballot measures, with more than half of school budgets tied to Sacramento–income tax, sales tax and corporate taxes. The Great Recession created what Joanne Faryon, a KPBS-TV political reporter called a ballooning affect: "Lower property taxes, lower income taxes, less money for the state, less money for the county, and education really ends up suffering because of it."

Yet the Golden State was the national leader back in 1960 when it passed its groundbreaking Master Plan for Higher Education. Developed by the legendary University of California President Clark Kerr and a team appointed by the UC Regents and the State Board of Education, the plan laid out an accessible and affordable roadmap to college for millions of Californians. The top 12.5 percent of high school graduates were eligible for entry into the University of California; the top third were eligible to enter the California State University system; and "anyone over eighteen years of age who could benefit from post-secondary education" was eligible to attend a community college.

For the next five decades higher education in California blossomed. In 2008, public and non-public enrollment totaled more than 3.9 million students. Roughly 650,000 attended a public university with 1.5 million in the extensive public community college system.

Fast-forward to the Great Recession; there were no shields adequate to defray direct hits on the enterprise of higher education. The California college fleet suffered significant, unprecedented and debilitating flack at all levels.

At the University of California ten-campus system, things are in turmoil. Funding from Sacramento in FY 2010 was reduced by $800 million–25 percent. There were student protests as student fees (what would be called tuition in most universities) were raised by 32 percent so that an entering freshman at UC Berkley in the fall of 2010 paid $11,000. That's a long, long way from the affordability envisioned in the fifty-year-old Master Plan. (In 1960, UC fees were $147.) And UC President Mark Yudof has been forced to make other decisions not popular with anyone: layoffs, furloughs, reduced course offerings. When *TIME* magazine ran a story naming him as "one of the nation's top ten educational leaders," a flood of protest emails inundated its office.

It has been much the same picture in the twenty-three campus California State University system, as discussed in Chapter I. Facing a $600 million reduction (20 percent), Chancellor Charles Reed slapped a cap on system enrollment, denying entry to 40,000 students for FY 2010 and that cap will be re-imposed in FY 2011. As with UC, there have been furloughs, layoffs and protests as tuition, which had already gone up by 20 percent was likely to be increased by another 10 percent in 2010-11.

California's 110 community Colleges have also felt the pain. Their 8 percent cut in state funding was the largest in history. Chancellor Jack Scott estimates that 200,000 students may not be able to enroll in FY 2011.

Let's go back to the Pew Center report (referenced to earlier in this Chapter), because it has a second significant dimension. The study found that nine other states were following closely on California's heels: Arizona, Nevada, Oregon, Michigan, Illinois, Wisconsin, New Jersey and Rhode Island. These ten states comprise more than a third of the US population and economic output. To make matters worse, a handful of other states were uncomfortably close behind: Colorado, Georgia, Kentucky, New York, and Hawaii. All together, these states make up half the US population.

Between FY 1999 and FY 2009, spending on higher education rose, on average, about 50 percent across the nation. The highest increased percentage in the nation was in Wyoming (125 percent), but a sharp change of direction started to occur in FY 2008. Although a few states (Alaska, Texas, North Dakota and Wyoming) escaped first-year gouging, there has been a downward avalanche since for state tax coffers. In their July 2010 State Budget Update, the National Conference of State Legislatures reported that collectively the states were facing fiscal 2011 budget gap of $84 billion. "More gaps are expected in the next two years," and Executive Director William Pound is not optimistic about the future. "It will be a long march before state revenues return to their pre-recession levels, not to mention other hurdles lawmakers have to clear."

What should not be missed in this horror story is that "Jaws II" is coming. Remember the scene in the movie *Jaws* when Roy Schneider is standing on a small fishing boat and finally sees the gigantic shark take a sizable bite out of the back of the boat. Part in awe and part in fear he utters, "We are going to need a BIGGER boat!" In the case of higher education today, though, we may need a life raft.

Every state in the union including South Carolina (whose governor did not want to take the money), has defrayed deep cuts by way of federal stimulus dollars. A few states chose to use the money over three years; most over two. Florida, Georgia and Virginia went "all in" during year one. Although there is always a possibility of more stimulus funds (like the fifth $38 billion federal extension for unemployment benefits), even differently labeled federal funding initiatives are growing politically unpopular and the outcomes of the November 2010 elections may have put a stop to them altogether.

Higher education has made some typical (albeit temporary) moves such as freezing open positions, curtailing classes, upping tuition, and furloughing or laying off employees. In California, that has not gone well. There have been student protests over the sharp increases in tuition, including one at University House (the campus home of UC Berkeley Chancellor Robert Birgeneau) where 70 students assembled, chanted, and smashed windows and lights. Some of the emotions were caused by poor decisions. UC students were shell-shocked by the 32 percent two-year increases in tuition, and faculty and staff were upset at the layoffs and furloughs (actually pay cuts because employees were not paid for mandated days off).

With all of that going on, news media regularly highlighted a series of frivolous things that should or could have been cut. *The Los Angeles Times* headlined that "State Universities Tap Student Fees for Unintended Projects" such as construction, real estate losses and even "loans to high ranking officials." The *San Francisco Chronicle* revealed that while thousands were furloughed, the number of staff earning over $214,000 had risen by more than 6 percent. Others had benefited from "lucrative overtime pay" or "incentive pay." Indeed, the general public even wanted to cut off their water; it seems that in spite of all the need to cutback on education expenses, the University of California was still spending $2 million annually on bottled water. Later it was revealed that UC faced an unfunded pension gap equaling its annual budget. One of the key factors? No contribution from the institution or the employees for the past nineteen years!

No wonder then that, with a Field Poll showing that for three years running Californians had seen themselves becoming "worse off financially"–with nineteen in twenty residents saying the Golden State economy was in "bad times"–there is not great support for new dollars for public higher education. When the Public Policy Institute of California asked via a statewide survey, 41 percent of likely voters said that colleges and universities should "use existing funds more wisely."

And, as we have already noted, what's happening in California is unfolding across the rest of the nation: Massachusetts reduced its FY 2011 public-college support by 15 percent; Mississippi cut 13 percent; Louisiana by 20 percent during the previous eighteen months; and in Illinois postsecondary education lost $100 million. Michigan has cut higher education appropriations for seven years in a row. Georgia's University System lost 10 percent of its state support for the new fiscal year and anticipates additional cuts of up to 8 percent during the year. Utah cut its support for higher education by 24 percent between 2008 and 2010. In response, tuition rates at pubic colleges and universities are zooming higher: the North Carolina university system is up 15 percent; Alabama A&M is up 23 percent; and the University of Washington is up 30 percent.

A few states are making baby steps toward meaningful long-term higher educational reform. Connecticut offered early retirement and 250 professors accepted. Rhode Island consolidated a large number of college majors. Ohio moved closer to performance-based funding. New Mexico and Utah are offering more bachelor's degrees via community colleges. Indiana is aiming to do more with online education. Maine is exploring three-year bachelor's degrees.

Fifty states and 4,400 colleges and universities: How many will continue to use smoke and mirrors while simply trying to "muddle through?" The old stand-by of kicking the can down the road and waiting for Godot will no longer do. What we need is structural, scalable change *away* from the historical unsustainable university model. We simply can't afford to keep trotting out the tired old paradigm.

Change? Yes, indeed. And we need to put on some speed**!**

Chapter IX

# AMERICA'S COLLEGE

"This is the moment for Community Colleges."
Jill Biden

It was August 1957, and three East Detroit high school graduates were embarking for sunny California. Ron, Ken and I left Michigan early Monday morning and drove a 1951 Chevy some 2,700 miles in fifty-eight hours. We took turns sleeping and driving, stopping only for food and gasoline. Like millions of fortune seekers and tourists who headed west, we followed old Route 66. We cruised under the St. Louis Arch, roasted under the hot Mohave desert sun, and got hair cuts and ninety-nine-cent full breakfasts in Las Vegas at four o'clock in the morning. We hung out at Hollywood and Vine. We took in the handprints and footprints of the stars at Mann's (now Grauman's) Chinese Theatre.

After staying with Ken's in-laws in Los Angeles, we drove the hundred miles to Taft. We had all been part of our Michigan high school's undefeated football team and were on our way to attend the small California Junior College located there via football scholarships. In what were known as "two-a-days," the 110 degree temperature caused us to work out at six in the morning and then again at seven at night. As classes started, I received some ominous news. Since my writing skills were not "up to par," I would be taking something known as "English R" (remedial English).

At that time I did not know much about college. After my first class on Monday, I actually went back to the same classroom Tuesday morning at the same time. I did not know that college classes did not meet five days a week. I was the first member of my family to attend college. The subject had gotten little attention at home or in my high school. I hadn't read more than a handful of books and we rarely had been assigned homework. Other than a last-minute decision to attend the junior college in California, my plan after high school was to go to work on one of Detroit's automobile-assembly lines "making big bucks."

That first semester at Taft Junior College changed my life. I would go on to finish the year, then transfer to Detroit's Wayne State University where I would acquire two degrees. Later, a PhD from Purdue University would follow .Then, after a stint of seven years as a college assistant professor and director of debate, I ran for the Michigan Legislature, got elected, and served for six years.

The next step? Twenty years after leaving that small community college campus, I would be returning to one. . .as president. It would be my pleasure to serve as president of three community colleges over the next fifteen years: California's Imperial Valley College was rural with 5,000 students; Citrus College (also in California) was a suburban college with 10,000 students; and Austin Community College (Texas) was a large urban college of more than 20,000.

Just as community college had changed my life, I wanted to help make that grand transition possible for thousands of others. My roots to the community-college movement run deep. Even with the recent national administration push, this sector of higher education is not fully understood, appreciated, or financially well-supported. Yet it is an ingrained part of the higher education landscape.

In 1907, California lawmakers allowed for high schools to add a thirteenth and fourteenth grade and that became a normal pattern. (To this day the title "California Community College president" carries with it the old K-12 baggage "president and superintendent.") Three different currents of change generated this uniquely American institution. First, the economic "Panic of 1893" had caused people to wonder if they could afford the four-year universities and whether or not everyone needed a four-year education. Creating a two-year college terminal degree provided a more economical alternative. Second, some of the leading university presidents of that era wanted to establish a clear distinction between the purpose of a college, which they saw as teaching the core liberal arts, and the purpose of a university, which was seen as the advancement of knowledge and research. Third, as a result of compulsory and growing K-12 educational needs, junior colleges became a major source for training teachers.

Up until the Great Depression the major focus of these "new-fangled institutions" was to prepare students for a terminal two-year degree or prepare them for transfer to a four-year college for their junior and senior years of instruction. Hence the common label, "junior college." The term seemed doubly appropriate since many of these institutions were separating from their former high school attachment. As the industrial age took hold, and after the massive unemployment experienced during the Great Depression, a second focus was added to the community college mission: developing "semi-professionals" for the workforce. Two of the major boosts for these two-year colleges (and for the entire national higher education system) occurred in the aftermath of World War II–the G.I. Bill and the Truman Commission Report.

The Servicemen's Readjustment Act of 1944 (the G.I. Bill) granted college or vocational benefits for returning veterans. The huge number of post-war veterans created massive need for new college capacity. Over the life of the original legislation (which has been extended in one form or another until the present time) 8 million veterans took advantage of the educational incentives. A large number of them chose community colleges. In 1946, President Henry Truman appointed a Presidential Commission on Higher Education "to reexamine our system of higher education in terms of its objectives, methods, and facilities: and in the light of the social role it has to play." In 1947, the Truman Commission presented the nation with a half dozen recommendations. All six argued for a larger role for the nation's community colleges. In fact, one commission recommendation emphatically stated: "The time has come to make education through the fourteenth grade available in the same way that high school is now available."

The report went on to declare that the two-year colleges needed to be developed "much more extensively than at present" and that "the services they perform be recognized and vastly extended." Finally, the commission concluded that "community colleges would have to carry a large part of the responsibility for expanding opportunities in higher education." Looking out a baker's dozen years, the commission anticipated that by 1960, 46 million "young people" would be enrolled in higher education and anticipated that 2.5 million of them would be enrolled at the junior college level!

In the mid-1960s, Congress passed the Higher Education Act of 1965 as a major part of President Lyndon Johnson's Great Society Agenda. The legislation was historic in that it established federal financial aid for students seeking a college degree. (That 1965 Act has been amended and extended eight times.) As a result of these historic legislative actions and the needs and wants of our society, the uniquely American two-year college has grown and expanded in both mission and number of students served.

The present-day expanded mission includes transfer, vocational and career education, certificates and degrees, noncredit offerings, dual-enrolled high school students, retraining programs, remedial education, community services, reversed degree students (those who already have a bachelor's degree or higher), and even the granting of bachelor's degrees in limited fields.

And the numbers? They are mind-blowing. Between 1963 and 2006 community-college enrollment grew by 740 percent compared to 200 percent for four-year institutions and 170 percent at private four-year colleges. And between 2007 and 2009, two show-stopping things happened: first, despite the Great Recession, community college enrollment in credit courses actually grew by 17 percent; second, full-time credit enrollment increased by a startling 24 percent. In 2008, credit enrollment at community colleges numbered more than 7 million students and 44 percent of the nation's undergraduates were enrolled at community colleges. And the two-year sector is expected to continue to grow by 20 percent during the next decade.

As the economic picture worsened, Americans voted with their feet. When people lost jobs (or became concerned they would lose their jobs) they followed a historic pattern and went back to college. A large reason for the two-year choice was the average cost of tuition and fees. The choice seemed more than understandable: pay $2,400 to attend a two-year college, or $7,000 to attend a public four-year college, or approximately six times that to an expensive for-profit institution–not to mention the average private college cost of $26,000.

But the solution of attending a community college was rapidly reaching a demand vs. financial capacity wall. As state coffers dwindled, so did the financial support for higher education. Students who could not get the classes they wanted were put on a holding list or were simply not allowed to register. The seventy-two-district California Community Colleges system, comprising the largest system of higher education in the US, was forced to reduce course offerings by 6 percent after losing 8 percent of its state funding. The pattern of less revenue chasing more students made its impact in the vast majority of the states. From Clackamas Community College in Oregon to Virginia's Bunker Hill Community College, a thundering herd of students was squeezed out of the four-year world and sought refuge at the community colleges as the economy continued downward. Demand could not match money, courses and space available.

Meanwhile, the was great hope in Mudville (higher education) when the mighty Casey (President Obama) came to the plate. Everyone believed that his bat was not cork-centered and his thin frame exhibited no steroids. His previously unblemished batting ability promised a new frontier of sorts for higher education and for community colleges in particular. And Obama came forth proposing an educational moon shot. He first envisioned a $2.5 billion College Access and Completion Fund. He encouraged everyone to commit to a year or more of college or job training and set a goal that by 2020 our nation would again boast the highest proportion of college graduates in the world. He labeled America's community colleges as underappreciated, underutilized, and (with shades of John F. Kennedy) said that degree-wise they were not "operating at full capacity."

The focus of national attention grew beyond the tandem of "A" words–Access and Affordability–and expanded to include a critical new "A" word: **Attainment** (completion of college). The attainment of a degree is truly a new national concern. In fact, graduation-rate data were not collected by the Department of Education until fifteen years ago, focuses mainly on undergraduates, and emphasizes six-year attainment numbers. This was the result of reports that other nations were getting ahead–and in fact already were ahead of the US in terms of degrees and certificates in higher education. A new "degree gap" awareness has now gained the attention of the nation.

To fill that "degree gap" President Obama also called for an American Graduation Initiative which would provide $12 billion over the next decade in order to deliver 5 million more degrees from the nation's two-year colleges. He planned to secure the funds for this effort (and more) by prying federal student loans from the hands of banks and lenders, and mandating that all federal student aid would be provided through a Department of Education Direct Loan Program.

The idea seemed solid (unless you were a current lender) and the funds at stake were gigantic. A switch from governmental subsidies to banks for guaranteed student loans to direct government loans was projected to save nearly $70 billion over the next decade. That money could be spent on other urgently needed items, such as reducing the deficit, providing for health care or new investments in higher education. And President Obama clearly adhered to the two-year colleges as the core of his degree-attainment plans. The battle over direct governmental lending was not an easy one, but in the end a combination of factors tipped the scale: the economy was in the ditch; the president's party was in control; the banks were not in good public standing; and the goal seemed worthy. In late March 2010, after a truly brutal battle over health care, the president signed legislation that achieved the changeover to direct lending.

But politics being politics, the Health Care and Education Reconciliation Act of 2010 did not produce the $12 billion for degree attainment. Instead, the community colleges received $2 billion over four years "to provide, improve, and develop education and career training programs." The community colleges did, however, receive something more valuable– the focus of national attention on a scale not seen since the Truman Commission some sixty years earlier. Always seen as central to access and affordability, they now were seen by both Washington and the public as the focal point for degree attainment.

The President tapped Jill Biden (wife of Vice President Joe Biden) to host a White House Summit on Community Colleges in October 2010, and made it clear that the $2 billion was only a down payment toward his

$12 billion promise. Jill Biden was the perfect choice. A community college professor herself–she teaches English at Northern Virginia Community College–she laments that the "sizable and valuable contributions" of these 1,200 colleges are not widely known, acknowledged or appreciated. While President Obama seeks a legitimate means "to innovate and educate our way to a better economy," Biden saw the summit as an opportunity to "shine a spotlight on one of higher education's best kept secrets." The White House Summit attracted more than a hundred community college leaders, three cabinet secretaries and several agency staff. Although no new dollars were forthcoming, the national stage provided an opportunity to respond to some severe criticism that had emanated from the for profit sector.

Earlier in the year, Senate Hearings, a sting operation by the Governmental Accounting Agency, and a Department of Education rule regarding "gainful employment" had focused negative public attention on the for profit sector. In response that sector got busy with a counter-information blitz. Full-page ads were placed in national newspapers; a gigantic effort was launched urging students to write their congressmen; the sector doubled down by hiring more agents for their DC lobby stable; and public as well as private nonprofit institutions of higher education were warned that any new DOE rulings would eventually apply to them. One mistake made, though, was criticizing the public community colleges for "unsavory recruitment practices, poorer-than-expected academic quality, course availability, class scheduling, job placement and personal attention." Not surprisingly, the American Association of Community Colleges shot back with a loaded gun–a fifteen-page policy brief concluding that "the two sectors [community colleges and for-profits] are far from being close kin."

Although the response to the for-profit sector claims to be written "not to win a debate or to suggest public policy," it does both. Key differences include governance, financing, student loans, profit vs. nonprofit, and marketing. While community colleges report to a public governmental appointed or elected body that is focused on a broad public mission, the for-profits report to their owners or stockholders on a much more narrowed mission. Also, public community colleges receive state and local tax support, while the private sector relies heavily on federal student loans. In FY 2008, only 10 percent of public two-year colleges utilized federal loans compared to nearly 90 percent in the for-profit sector. Loan default rates favor the community colleges, as well. The community colleges are nonprofit while the for-profit sector must grow each year to increase their profit margin. That is one reason their spending on marketing and advertising dwarfs that spent by their public competitors by a ration of 30 percent vs. 3 percent. Taking on the community colleges was and is a gigantic mistake. There are community colleges in virtually all congressional districts and the president and vice president are big fans.

Make no mistake; this *is* the time for the American community-college movement. Higher education can no longer paint by the numbers. The future will call for bold new strokes. The road out of recession calls for new constructs–the ability to adapt, change and break the mold. And what other segment of higher education has continually shown the capability to enlarge its mission in service to the public over the last 100 years? Our four-year universities haven't changed much in their basic structure, organization, or purpose over the last century. A former General Motors vice president put it this way, "University speed is deceptive. They are much slower than they look." Not so with our community colleges. Originally created as a bridge between high school and college, they are continually transitioning and transforming themselves as the needs of our nation dictated toward transfer, vocational instruction, community service and much more. And they do the task at a bargain rate.

Just ten years ago Florida became the first state to allow a community college to offer a bachelor's degree. That innovation boomed over the last decade and is now practiced in seventeen states. Florida community colleges currently offer 111 baccalaureate degrees in areas such as nursing, science management and education. In fact, a new state law passed in 2010 that will allow any two-year college that has offered a four-year degree for the past three years to petition for new four-year degree authority to make that decision themselves.

The major forces birthing the two-year college was the "Panic of 1893" and economic need continues to drive the movement from agricultural to industrial, to service, to digital as our society evolves.

In terms of educating and training our nation, it's important to ask three questions:

Who answered the call for access and affordability?

Who stands best suited to provide the certificates and degree attainment needed for America to continue world leadership?

Where can our nation obtain the best bang for the buck?

The answer to all three: **The American Community College!**

Chapter X
# SKIING BAREFOOT

Each is given a bag of tools,
A shapeless mass,
A book of rules;
And each must make–
Ere life is flown–
A stumbling block
Or a stepping stone.
R.L. Sharpe

I was twenty years old and had never been waterskiing. Truth be told, I am not a water enthusiast. But my Alpha Sigma Phi fraternity brothers told me how great it was and urged me to give it a try. So one warm, summer Saturday, I decided to do it. To my great surprise it wasn't all that difficult. On my third try, I was "up" for a full ten minutes. "If that was so easy, my friend Gordy said, "Why don't you try it on one ski?" *Why not?* I asked myself. And I did, flopping flat on my face at least a dozen times. Finally I admitted defeat, at least for the moment. Later, while we were sitting at a picnic table enjoying some refreshments, Gordy deadpanned, "Do you think we should tell him about the *special* ski?" Turns out they were enjoying my continual flopping around so much that they hadn't bothered to share the fact that when slalom skiing, it helps to have the special single, much wider ski made for the task!

here is a lesson here for higher education: If you are facing a new situation with a greater degree of difficulty, it might be wise to restock your tool box.

Having been the CEO of six colleges and universities over the past thirty years, I can tell you that there is a standard "two ski" tool kit for dealing with shortfalls in the budget. It doesn't matter whether the cause is a drop in state funding, investment loss, a sharp downturn in fund raising, or some other source. But instead of a hammer, screwdriver, pliers and adjustable wrenches, the standard tool chest at academic institutions includes travel reductions, attrition, borrowing, increases in tuition and fees (remember, US airlines collected almost $8 billion in fees in 2009), delaying maintenance, buy outs, early retirement incentives, increasing the spending rate of the endowment, upping fund-raising efforts, recruiting more out-of-state or international students (who pay much higher tuition rates that the institutions get to keep), freezing positions, eliminating part-time faculty, decreasing the number of full-time staff, and only as a last resort laying off full-time and tenured faculty.

There are even minor tinkering tools. The University of Florida is saving water by banning serving trays when students dine on campus. Students living in dormitories at Texas A&M are now buying their own toilet paper. At George Washington University, maid service has been suspended.

Schools like Sweet Briar College jacked up their discount rate to 42 percent (7 percent more than what is considered the upper margin of prudence), and have even allowed their endowment payout rate to go as high as 10 percent (about double the norm). But those tools are *not* sustainable.

On an academic campus the procedure is vastly different from a typical business reduction in force. The president does not simply select which tools he or she thinks best. Instead of proceeding with a clear and concise snap, crackle and pop plan–whether it be by tradition, past practices, expectation, or union necessity–there has to be a broad consultation or even a bargaining process involving all campus constituents. That scenario is one of the reasons that even this standard "two ski" tool kit is difficult to utilize effectively.

All of these "two ski" tools have been developed with an expectation that the downturn is temporary and that "things will get back to normal." But what if they don't? What if the reduction is of longer duration? Then, it is time to do more with less and select more modern and relevant tools. After all, we don't still use slide rules, typewriters, and snail mail. As a general strategy, the old "muddling through" may simply amount to rearranging the chairs on the deck of the Titanic.

Although "one ski" tools have been available for a half century (and developed, assembled, and implemented) in the world of business, these newer tools have not found broad acceptance in academia. The "one ski" kit contains things like outsourcing, benchmarking, furloughs, reducing retirement and health benefits, mergers, and even selling (out?) university accreditation.

Let's go a bit further. What if the economic bad news is not short-term? What if What if the gravy years are gone? What if the current situation is permanent? Then, the unthinkable: it's time to move beyond the "two ski" and "one ski" tool kits. Then it's time to learn how to ski barefoot.

Higher education is going to have to be much more adept and skilled in utilizing what we call "Tools for Tomorrow." We already have the tools; the problem is finding the courage to use them.

The "barefoot-ski" tool kit contains many items familiar to the legislative world: grandfathering, pilot projects, phase-ins, sun-setting, spending caps, triggers, virtual privatization, delayering, partnerships, economy commissions, spans of empowerment, setting targets, getting rid of sacred cows and taking advantage of crises.

**Grandfathering:** No employee expects things that were promised to be taken away. That's insensitive, cold, and an uphill battle. If you seek to change something no longer affordable, stipulate that the reduced salary or benefit will only affect new employees. Michigan State University used this gentle rubber mallet in making the decision not to offer retiree health benefits to faculty and staff hired after July 1, 2010. Purdue University grandfathered its decision to reduce pension-match amounts for new employees. Washington, DC and state governments have been using this tool for years. Hundreds of state and local pension-reform efforts are utilizing this powerful tool. It's time for universities to discover it and take action to control future spending.

**Piloting:** Before launching a full-scale program for textbook leasing in place of outright purchases, Follett conducted a pilot test at seven of its college bookstores. The test saved students $2 million in the cost of new textbooks. Golden Gate University students are now saving money permanently under this arrangement.

After restricting online offerings to its extension courses, where a bare 6 percent count toward credit at the university, a landmark pilot program is underway at the University of California in which $6 million in private funds will be used to create up to forty courses for online degree credit. The long-range goal is to offer full undergraduate degrees (or at minimum, the first two years) via the Internet. If the pilot effort is successful, UC hopes to be the first premier public university in the nation to do so. (A similar attempt at the University of Illinois, however, has already failed.)

**Phase-Ins:** The new national health -are reform law passed in 2010 is a Mona Lisa example–this landmark legislation extends health-insurance coverage to 32 million Americans who have been unable to get health insurance in the past. The first pieces of the program began in July 2010 with the requirement that each state offer temporary coverage for high-risk citizens who have preexisting conditions. In September 2010 insurance companies were no longer able to cap policies with lifetime limits. By 2014, when most of the extensive provisions kick in, plans must spend at least 85 percent of premiums collected on medical care. The total program will not be in place until 2020.

And what about the billions in savings that are supposed to accompany the law? It matters in terms of who provides the numbers. Although the White House predicts that the program will reduce the deficit by $140 billion over the next decade, you might want to inspect the math. After all, adding 32 million people and saving $140 billion does not seem to square with reality. As a matter of fact, it doesn't.

Patricia Barry, writing in the *AARP Bulletin,* provides a quick lesson in Medicare math: the "savings" are actually "lower future increases." She explains that Medicare spending that averaged 8 percent over the past two decades is projected to grow by only 6 percent under the new program, according to the Congressional Budget Office. Like magic, that's how almost $400 billion of the "savings" are calculated. Likewise, another $200 billion "savings" is credited to "smaller increases in payments to hospitals, nursing homes, health workers and other medical providers." Maybe the application of this tool in this instance should be seen as the chisel.

Over the next decade, we will be able to judge how well the program has been phased in and if the estimated savings was even in the ballpark. One thing is sure though, the long-tailed phase-in does get politicians through several election cycles.

**Sun-setting:** This "hammer" is a firm deadline date when a program stops. Two current federal examples are the Salary Subsidy Program scheduled to sunset on September 30, 2010 and a package of huge tax cuts due to expire December 31, 2010.

The Salary Subsidy Program provided for unemployed parents to receive full wages paid by the feds as long as the companies they work for put up a 20 percent match (benefits for the workers). And according to the bipartisan Policy Center, the "Bush Tax Cuts" amounted to $3 trillion over the previous ten years (70 percent of the tax breaks were going to "regular working people."

At minimum, a sunset provision makes it necessary to re-examine a program and forces a decision as to whether or not it should be continued. That is usually a fifty-fifty chance. On such issues as the two cited above, elected officials often find themselves torn between the carrot (such as the need to exit the recession) and the consequences (for example, public anger over the growing national debt).

**Caps:** When the Board of Trustees of the Connecticut State University System decided to grant pay raises of more than 10 percent to the system's top executives, Governor Jodi Rell literally hit the ceiling, saying, "Frankly, I am at a loss to understand why, in these difficult times, the trustees would approve increases as much as 10 percent for people who are paid between $285,000 and $360,000 a year." The board backed down and approved the ceiling the governor had imposed.

New Jersey Governor Chris Christie placed a 4 percent cap on tuition and fees in 2010. Missouri Governor Jay Nixon said, "We simply can't continue to subsidize the choice to attend a private school," and wanted to cap such public payments to private colleges at zero. Meanwhile in Oklahoma, several legislators sought to cap the rapid rise in tuition by stipulating how much and when fee increases could be imposed.

There also is grave concern in many states that salaries and pensions for public employees are totally out of control. A 2010 Cato Institute Study found that local and state compensation and benefits were substantially higher than for similar jobs in the private sector. Average salaries for state and local workers were reported being $67,812 vs. less than $60,000 for those in the private sector workforce. And in California, public pensions that cost the state $1 billion a decade earlier today cost $5 billion. A cap could be set by a new formula or changing over to an undefined benefit plan.

There is more bad news at the national level. The average federal employee receives almost twice the amount of the average private-sector worker in terms of salary and benefits: $111,000 vs. $60,000, according to a recent Heritage Foundation study. And a *USA Today* analysis in August 2010 supported an even larger gap: $123,000 vs. $61,000 adding, "Federal workers have been awarded bigger average pay and benefit increases than private employment for nine years in a row." Dennis Cauchon also noted, "The compensation gap between federal and private workers has doubled in the past decade." We are also hiring more federal workers during the Great Recession. Bureau of Labor Statistics data show 250,000 jobs added since July 2007. Instead of more public employees, higher pay and higher public-pension benefits, why not impose a ceiling? Even free-spending President Obama froze bonuses for 2,900 senior political appointees. This mismatch of resource allocation is simply not sustainable.

**Triggers:** Circumstances change. As an example, this tool can certify that— if the economy goes south— certain steps will be taken to balance the books. Former California Governor Arnold Schwarzenegger listed a series of such automatic corrective actions in his January 2010 state budget address in case revenue projections didn't hold. (In California with its finances constantly shifting, such an observation is a little like Ivory soap:

9.44 percent certain!)

In spite of public outrage over the Troubled Asset Relief Program (TARP), and the initial $1.6 billion bailout for seventeen firms, Kenneth Feinberg, the Obama Administration's initial watchdog over executive compensation, called for only prospective, non-retroactive action. Feinberg said he was "trying to minimize the likelihood" that his decision would "trigger another round of investigations and litigation."

**Virtual Privatization:** In confirmation of the fact that the proportion of state spending for higher education has been declining for years, university officials frequently offer up this thumbnail history: "In the beginning there were state-*funded* universities. Then state-*supported* universities. Then state-*assisted* universities. Now, after thirty-two months of recession, there are only state-*located* universities."

Historically, as state funding receded, there has always been an informal agreement by which state legislators would allow tuition to climb as state funding for other priorities such as health care, welfare and prison needs grew. As state coffers have dwindled there has been talk of privatization; and the case makes some sense. The University of Colorado, for example, receives a meager 3.3 percent of its operating budget from the state legislature. Although total independence is unlikely, virtual privatization that allows frontline state universities to set their own tuition while maintaining less state control, seems a reasonable compromise (although there are some harmful side effects).

In New York, Governor David Paterson proposed in January 2010 that the State University of New York and the City University of New York be allowed to set their own tuition rates and keep the money the fees would generate. Support for that position was encouraged with a rumored pledge of $150 million by James Simons, one of the world's financial elite. Simons, however, would only make the gift if the sixty-four components of the State of New York were authorized to raise tuition without having to seek approval from the legislature.

**Delayering:** Make no mistake; reducing the number of management levels in academia is both needed and doable. Here it is time to use the cudgel. The number of staff and administrators has gotten way out of hand and there is great opportunity to thin out the ranks.

"Colleges have added managers and support personnel at a steady, vigorous clip over the past twenty years, far outpacing the growth in student enrollment and instructors," according to Jeffrey Brainard data and statistics manager at the *Chronicle of Higher Education*. While instructional positions rose about 50 percent according to the Center for College Affordability and Productivity, support or back-office staff more than doubled. The center concluded that the ballooning support staff was clearly "unproductive spending by academe."

The Goldwater Institute reported in August 2010 that "administration is consuming a large and rapidly growing portion of university resources." In examining 200 of the nation's leading pubic and private universities the institute found that almost 40 percent of the full-time employees were in administration while fewer than 30 percent were involved in instruction, research and service. Patrick Callan of the National Center for Public Policy agrees that this development is "simply not a trend that's supportable." Richard Vedder, an economics professor at Ohio University who served on the Commission on the Future of Higher Education with Department of Education Secretary Margaret Spellings, said flatly, "It's time for higher education to go on a diet."

Evidence of this bloat is also overwhelmingly supported by the Delta Cost Project and the American Association of University Professors. The *Chronicle of Higher Education* has gone so far as to trace the nearly unbelievable disproportion of back-office staff at a number of universities.

vould think that some of these administrators didn't have a *Clue*! It wasn't Professor Plum in the library with the lead pipe; the crime has been committed by hiring a mob of unneeded support staff on numerous university campuses.

Not surprisingly, some of these positions are the first to go during an economic crisis. The University of San Francisco's restructuring plan calls for elimination of more than 500 positions over three years: central administration would shrink by thirty-five and research by double that, finance and human resources by 100 and IT by more than 200. But a large number of colleges are resorting to furloughs, simply putting off the problem. You have to wonder why all of these folks were hired in the first place. And then, why would they be furloughed and not just released. The new normal demands a swift change of thinking. If you have one of these too-high multi-layered cakes, it's high time to think in terms of flapjacks. USF: three years is way too long to wait!

**Partnerships:** Some universities are forging partnerships to advance their agenda. In Ohio, public universities are partnering with Procter & Gamble to speed up the invention-to-production process. Michigan universities are working with business groups to provide 25,000 internships.

**Economy Commissions:** In spring 2010 President Obama established a bipartisan, eighteen-member Deficit Reduction Commission. The president promised to endorse the commission's findings if fourteen of the members could agree on a particular proposal. This was necessary because the president did not want to absorb the political heat for making the recommendations on his own.

To stave off budget cuts state governments have been making moves such as merging or eliminating departments and centralizing operations. About a dozen states have utilized consulting panels to find ways to cut waste and inefficiencies. Florida's panel came up with more than eighty recommendations yielding savings of $3 billion. A Michigan model eliminated 300 boards. Outcome? Another $3 billion in savings. Likewise, some universities are taking advantage of this newfound tool. An outside firm identified $75 million worth of "bloat, waste and redundancy" at UC Berkeley. For example, there was one manager for every sixty-three employees in UCB Human Resources compared to an average of double that at other institutions. (And that assumes the average is the right level.)

**Span of Empowerment:** On the flipside of the delayering coin is the "Span of Empowerment." If the axiom is fewer layers of management, then the corollary must be more people managed by fewer people. Sticking with UC Berkeley, the consultants found the biggest area of bloat was too many managers. Do you really need five vice presidents, seven deans, five associate deans and three assistant deans, or a department chair for a three-person department? You get the picture.

**Targets:** A sharpshooter learned of a twelve-year-old boy who "hit the bull's eye" every time and decided to meet the extraordinary youngster. As the sharpshooter approached the boy, he observed some 100 targets with dead-center shots in every one. Shaking his head in disbelief, he asked the youngster, "How were you able to do that?" The boy replied, "Aw, it's not so difficult. I just shoot the hole and then draw the circle."

Defense Secretary Robert Gates recently decided to identify the targets and then shoot the holes. With Pentagon spending doubling in the last decade he identified nine "areas of opportunity" took aim and fired. Weapon systems were one of his targets and Secretary Gates eliminated the F-22 fighter jet designed for use in the Cold War era.

Although bloat is legendary in the military, the world of academia is also target- rich. Let's select one key target: campus construction. Between 2002 and 2008, US campuses went on a $93 billion construction binge! This, in spite of the fact that most buildings already sit empty during long semester breaks and the summer months every year. Not only that, but classrooms are more often empty than in use in every state every day. Wouldn't it make more sense to think in terms of three-year degrees, where students don't leave campus, don't have an extra year's expense, and don't have such a large amount of debt to repay? With dramatic online growth, what are colleges going to with the buildings that already exist such as dorms with twenty- or thirty-year bond debt? You might want to contact the state university of New York's Stony Brook's Southampton location where plans are underway to shutter a large number of buildings. And South Hampton is not alone–more than 1,000 small colleges and universities are going to have to buy a ton of mothballs over the next decade.

**Sacred Cows:** Perhaps the greatest need is for a tool that allows you to zap the untouchables that exist on university campuses. If you have ever been part of a traditional college campus, you know that every single thing has a loyal and vociferous support group. Campus culture assumes that *everything* has "intrinsic value" and should be allowed to "run along as it always has."

The University of Vermont has heard cow bells ringing for a long, long time, but this summer their College of Agriculture and Life Sciences plans to sell its herd of 255 Holsteins. Why? Low milk prices and high grain costs, teamed with university budget cuts. But they are not crying over the milk being spilled. Instead of owning their own cattle, the university plans to save money by working with the stock of private farm owners. Dean Tom Vogelmann is enthusiastic about the switch. In fact, he feels it could become a new model for land-grant institutions. He may be right: the

University of Michigan and the University of Minnesota are taking similar steps, and the University of Illinois is dropping fifty of its agricultural extension locations.

Easy enough. But let's go for a bigger thundering herd of sacred cows: college athletics. The Knight Commission has released a number of reports with two clear themes. First, the vast majority (more than 90 percent) of university athletics departments lose significant money. Second, university presidents don't have the support to slay the fire-breathing, athletic dragon. But as faculty anger, student awareness and public scrutiny expose the vast amount of student fees that are siphoned both directly and indirectly into the athletic monster's tank, there is hope. In this era of scarcity, "St. Crisis" may finally slay or at least disable the beast.

But the sacred cows are also numerous on the academic side of the institution. A large number of majors and disciplines aren't really necessary. More than 80 percent of baccalaureate institutions, 70 percent of master's institutions, and 40 percent of research institutions graduate fewer than seven students in one-fourth of their academic programs, according to David Glenn and Peter Schmidt of the *Chronicle of Higher Education*. In Nevada the State Board of Regents cut numerous departments and degree programs at both the Reno and the Las Vegas campuses in June 2010. That needs to happen across the board.

**Advantage Crisis:** Thomas Freidman, in his book *The World Is Flat* advises, "It is a shame to waste a good crisis." He is right. In demanding times, executives are given far more slack. Witness President Obama's overhaul of the financial regulations in 2010, labeled by the Associated Press as "the stiffest restrictions on banks and Wall Street since the Great Depression."

No doubt the "barefoot skier's" tool kit could be chocked-full with other new instruments, but the tool kit is only part of the story. We need leaders on campus who know of the tools, are skilled in their use, who believe that progress is worth the risk, and who have the backbone to take action. Strong boards of trustees must back their administrators in both words and deeds. Being a college trustee is no longer simply an honorary title.

Thinking back on my first waterskiing lesson, I have news for my old friend Gordy: we can't keep the needed tools a secret any longer. It is now necessary for institutions of higher education to toss their two skis and even move way beyond the wider one ski. Nothing less that barefoot skiing will do. We are going at a much faster speed and although the risk is great, the ship of state demands that we do it.

The task will be difficult but it's our era's "westerning" challenge, and as pioneers we must press on instead of circling our institutional wagons.

That's why we pay our trail bosses those big bucks!

# Part Three: The Way Forward

Chapter XI

# TOUCHING THE THIRD RAIL

"By almost any measure, the status quo isn't working."
Robert Hertzberg
California Forward

As a first-time passenger on the San Francisco Bay Area Rapid Transit (BART) train, I noticed the signs advising: "Do Not Touch the Third Rail." Seems that third rail is electrified and contact with it could be extremely hazardous to your health.

Although that is probably sound advice to BART passengers, it appears that the same message is written in indelible ink across the forehead of virtually every elected official. Whether at the federal, state or local level representatives of the people regularly exhaust their maneuvering manuals in order to avoid touching that rail. The third rail in politics is code for "the untouchables" or so-called "sacred cows." The politicos know that these areas could be extremely hazardous to their political health.

When the economy is booming, there is no reason to deal with hard issues. When times are less lucrative, there's always borrowing, redirecting funds, and band aid fixes. Simply kick the can down the road to the next political session. It's like appearing on *Face the Nation* or *Meet the Press* and speaking in platitudes for a half hour. I observed these lessons in political reality as a member of the Michigan Legislature.

Being a freshman lawmaker in the Michigan House of Representatives, I did not get my first, second or even third choice of committee assignments. As one of the youngest members, I was "naturally" assigned to the Retirement Committee. You could have loaded both my knowledge of and enthusiasm for the assignment into one small duffle bag. But the legislature works by areas of specialization and each bill is referred to a committee that must study, review, and "report the bill out," or it dies. Over the next couple of years I invested serious time and learned a great deal about pensions, such as vesting (when you accrue a right to funds) and whether a specific fund was adequately funded (if you could pay the bill when it comes due). During that six-year span on the Retirement Committee, I learned three important and startling things.

First, other than in the judicial and legislative area, most pension plans were underfunded. Second, as a general rule, the investment-return estimates were done on a best-possible-case scenario (inflated). And finally, every year the legislature was either adding to or liberalizing benefits.

Because that did not seem logical or sustainable to me, I was allowed to occupy the floor microphone and make my annual speech saying: "We cannot continue to go down that road." After my speech, the new or increased benefits would pass by a wide margin.

That was more than thirty years ago and I now realize that what was true then in Michigan is now true in cities, counties, states and Washington, DC. Pensions have been a political third rail or sacred cow for far too long.

All of Europe shrugged a bit in the past when learning that musicians, pastry makers, hairdressers and even masseurs could retire as early as fifty or fifty-five in Greece because their professions were deemed "arduous or unhealthy." They also experienced little heartburn when bullfighters in Spain could do the same. That changed somewhat when the European Union formed a shared currency, but it changed dramatically when the

Greek debt crisis hit. That European earthquake sent aftershocks throughout the financial world. But the follies in Greece and Spain are not unrelated to equally irresponsible actions in the USA.

Let's survey the state and national pension train wrecks.

In 1999, the California Public Employees Retirement System (CalPERs), the largest public-pension system in the nation with more than $200 billion in assets, forecasted that the Dow Jones Industrial Average would reach 25,000 by 2009. Eleven years later that prediction was a full 60 percent off the mark! CalPERS it seems has frequently made similar significant errors in judgment. As of December 2009, the fund had experienced an almost 50 percent loss in its real estate holdings, and lost $300 million when BP stock hit the skids after the Gulf of Mexico blow out in April 2010. But the CalPERS quagmire is only the tip of the iceberg.

In February 2010, the Pew Center on the States released a landmark report on state retirement systems. The major finding? As of June 30, 2008, a cumulative $1 trillion gap existed between the benefits pledged and the money needed to pay the piper. Experts generally consider a coverage level of 80 percent of obligations as acceptable, but Pew found twenty-one states with less than that in their coffers. Eight states had funding deficiencies of one-third or more and two (Illinois and Kansas) were at the bottom of the list. Of course that study was *before* the major impact of the Great Recession, so things have only worsened over the past two years–the Pew Center estimates 25 percent worse!

In August 2010 a national study by Joshua Rauh of the Northwestern University Kellogg School of Management estimated the gap between pension promises and payment ability to be $1 trillion even if all the states "uniformly eliminated generous early retirement deals and raised the retirement age to seventy-four." That study also assumed annual investment returns of 8 percent. Since all three of those variables are pie in the sky, there is in reality a multi-trillion-dollar gap between *actual* pension obligations and what is on the books, not to mention the debt that is growing daily.

Another log on the pension bonfire is the growing amount of double dipping, which occurs when public employees retire, draw their pensions, and then come back to work for full pay, often in the same position. *The Seattle Times* located 2,000 individual workers who were drawing both a salary *and* a state pension. One public higher education double-dipper had collected $700,000 in retirement benefits while drawing full state pay. Perhaps states should ban double dipping? I mean, *duh*!

As if the pension situation were not peril enough, the Pew study also examined health care and additional non-pension state obligations. That portrait was much darker. States were providing only $15 billion in non pension benefits, yet the Pew study calculated that more than $40 billion should have been set aside in 2008. Over the next twenty years as more baby boomers retire and live longer, that deep, deep hole is going to look a lot like peering into Mammoth Cave.

At the federal level, things are just as screwed up. Yet we are hiring many more federal workers and paying them more than ever. Arthur Bruzzome, President of BSI Capital Group in San Francisco notes that "Since the election of President Obama, the number of federal employees making over $150,000 a year has doubled. And that does not include overtime pay and bonuses. These increases will yield even more federal pensions accompanied by what taxpayers, will surely see as a gigantic hospital bill."

Now, let's take our untouchable list to school.

As we touched on in Chapter X, the number one sacred cow is athletics. Twenty years ago, the Knight Commission on Intercollegiate Athletics released a three-pronged report panning intercollegiate athletics for their low graduation rates, lack of attention to academic standards, and for operating outside of university oversight. Earlier this year, the commission reported that the "costs of competing in big-time intercollegiate sports have soared," calling the need for fiscal reform, "urgent." The report, *Restoring the Balance*, stated matter-of-factly, "in high-profile sports, tensions often surface between the core mission of universities and commercial values." And, although those tensions have always been beneath the surface, the recession brought the contrast of the two campus worlds (academic and athletic) into sharp focus. While the academic world has seen layoffs, salary freezes, furloughs, curtailment of classes, and in general had to make do with less, the collegiate athletic world has continued to live in "Fat City."

*College Sports 101*, an October 2009 Knight Commission report, pinpoints four basic problems with the current financials of big-time intercollegiate athletics. First, over the past ten years, expenditures have shot steadily upward. Second, spending has far outpaced athletic-department revenue. Third, athletic budgets are eclipsing academic budgets. Fourth, and perhaps the unkindest cut of all, university subsidies for athletic programs are growing. What exactly are athletic subsidies? College presidents and athletic directors prefer the term "allocated revenue" instead of "athletic-deficit fill-in money." Primary sources for the subsidies are student fees, governmental support, and institutional direct or indirect support.

Although there is big money in television revenue and ticket sales, over the past five years the average operating deficit for the Football Bowl Subdivision (FBS) colleges has grown to more that $8 million. A *USA Today* analysis in 2010 concluded that "more than $800 million in student fees and university subsidies are propping up athletic programs at the nation's top sports colleges."

The amount of money being spent on college athletics today is both unwarranted, and scandalous. Take a look at football coaching salaries. When Alabama and Texas played to determine who would be number one last year, the head coaches on the field were being paid $7 million. Each received sizable bonuses for the game and the University of Texas coach (who lost the game) had his salary boosted to $5.1 million (an action labeled "unseemly and inappropriate" by the UT Faculty Council.) The average big-time head football coach in 2009 received a base salary of $1.36 million. But wait! It gets worse. Assistant football coaches are also experiencing the good life. Many in the FBS earn more than $250,000 and some much more. Assistant coaches are also starting to receive multi-year contracts and other supplemental benefits formerly reserved for head coaches.

And the story is the same for big time college basketball.

No wonder that faculty and staff (and hopefully the public) are starting to call for some control to be put in place. At UC Berkeley, best known for student protests, the administration is starting to feel the anger of its faculty over athletic spending. Over the past two years the university has provided $14 million in supplemental income to the athletic program. Not only that, faculty are agitated about sizable loans made to the athletic department that have "been forgiven." Facing a campus deficit of $150 million, the Faculty Senate last November passed a resolution calling for an end to both the subsidies and the loans. In September 2010, the university cut baseball and four other team sports. Still, its athletic subsidy is expected to be $5 million per year.

Ohio University faculty called on its administration to "significantly reduce" the 75 percent subsidy of its athletic program. And at least one university is getting the message. In the fall of 2009, Northeastern University announced that it was dropping its football program after more than seventy years. What was even more impressive than the action was the reasoning: "The decision was not simply about saving money, it was about where the university should spend money." That is precisely the right question.

But it is difficult to curtail athletic spending. So difficult that college presidents have admitted they can't control it. Why? **Too much politics!**

When Mississippi Governor Haley Barbour suggested that the state's fifteen community colleges reduce their costs by downsizing or even eliminating their athletic spending, it raised a few eyebrows because the cost for community college athletics is so much lower than at big universities. But clearly now is the time to rein in the athletic sacred cow. And finally, battle lines are being drawn. Surely some of the funds going to million-dollar salaries, massive facilities and the rest could be redirected to the academic side of the house. Shouldn't athletics subsidize the university, rather than the other way around?

There are multiple bogies on the collegiate "untouchable" and "sacred cow" list. In fact, it's a target-rich environment. Does it make sense in this fast-changing environment to guarantee a job for thirty years? Do we need scads of college administrators in this computer-savvy world? Do we need MORE buildings when the ones we have stand underutilized? Does it make sense to make a major out of every college minor? Do we truly need 120 (or more) credit hours in order to graduate? For *all* degrees? For *any* degree? Could universities get equal or even better outcomes spending *less* money?

One afternoon in Roscoe, Texas, I was passing a defunct newspaper office when a sign in the window caught my eye:

> *"When you're green you grow;*
> *when you're ripe you rot."*

This isn't Denmark, but much of higher education is rotting. American higher education can only become green again by **touching the third rail**!

Chapter XII

# THE THREE-YEAR PUBLIC OPTION

"The American model is beginning to creak and groan
...higher education could be among
the next economic sectors to undergo
a massive restructuring like the banking industry."

James Duderstadt
Former President
University of Michigan

So where do we go from here?

Being willing to touch the "Third Rail" and having the right tools are both great, but beg the question of design: What is it that we most need to accomplish to fix the crisis in American higher education? There is no shortage of prescriptions for what ails American colleges and universities. However, most of these predictably identify the institution as the patient, rather than focusing on the student needs the institution should be serving, but is not.

Likewise, we do not lack for visions of the "University of the Future," but most of them come without an instructional manual or GPS showing us how to get there from here.

To seize the opportunity for designing a game-changing solution to

America's Graduation Gridlock, we must establish a clear understanding of exactly what needs are going unmet in higher education. Otherwise we are just trying to nail Jell-O to the wall. Our task is to design a substantive response that will embody the precise job to be done–one that creates an unmistakable customer "value proposition" that becomes, to paraphrase *The Godfather*, "an offer that society can't refuse."

In previous Chapters we've discussed how starting with a societal perspective as a reference point for our design work is a good idea when it comes to identifying the most serious unmet educational needs. For example, we know that we are not producing enough associate, bachelor, and master degree recipients to meet the requirements of our society. Most future jobs will require at least two years of college-level learning and 40 percent will require a full undergraduate degree. Yet we are falling so far short of these known metrics that it is now taking six years or longer to even get to first base in terms of college completion rates. (Only 27 percent of students at public colleges and 48 percent at private schools finish a bachelor's degree in four years.) The US needs a response that covers all the three "A's" (accessibility, affordability and attainment) as well as the two "F's" (fast and flexible).

The United States is no longer a leader even in terms of associate's degrees, according to OCED. We ranks fifth (well behind Russia and Canada) in the percentage of adults (ages twenty-five to sixty-five) with at least an associate's degree and tenth for young adults (ages twenty-five to thirty-four). That is well behind Canada's 55 percent level of completion through the associate degree. China now leads the world with 25 million students enrolled in higher education institutions, and is taking in more students from abroad than it sends overseas (even though it now sends more university students to the US than India).

The deterioration in even the lowest level of college degree completion is probably due to the fact that the US student population which is growing the fastest (Hispanics) now suffers the lowest participation rate in higher education overall, as well as a poverty rate exceeding 30 percent, highest among all ethnic groups.

Sandy Baum, a higher education specialist at the College Board, put the challenge this way in an August 27, 2010, article: "Only by getting more young people from historically disadvantaged groups to prepare for, to enter, and to succeed in postsecondary education, and by meeting the even more daunting challenges of helping adults who missed out on college find a way back in, can further strides be made in our nation's educational attainment."

The US Department of Labor projections through to 2016 show that fifteen of the thirty fastest-growing occupations will require a full bachelor's degree or more. And occupations that require at least some post-high-school vocational certification or an associate's degree will account for 2.3 million additional jobs. By 2020, there will be an estimated 15 million new American jobs that will require a bachelor degree, according to the Council for Adult and Experiential Learning. But at our current pace we will show only about 3 million workers with baccalaureate credentials by that time. We also know, according to a report for the Council on Graduate Schools and the Educational Testing Service, that between now and 2018 the number of jobs requiring graduate degrees will grow by 2.5 million, a 17 percent increase.

For the first time in our history, in the words of President Michael Crow of Arizona State University, we are risking broad decline as a nation "as a consequence of the insufficient evolution of our institutions and the disinvestment that characterizes our policies toward higher education."

Many who are concerned with US higher education seem to at least perceive the repercussions of the Great Recession as opportunities, not just a curse. However, Crow also notes that their responses have consisted mainly of efforts to become more efficient or to hasten the return of "normalcy." He senses that these responses are inherently misguided. Why? Because, as he explains, "long before the economy proved that our sense of mastery over the course of events was not fully justified, American higher education had been marked not by advancement or even equilibrium but rather an ossification. . .[and] the lack of innovation in the organization and practices of our institutions."

Crow believes that "those of us in the academy are ourselves responsible for tolerating and perpetuating design flaws in our colleges and universities. Unless we come to appreciate the extent and severity of these design flaws, as well as the shortcomings in our overall model of higher education, our best efforts to turn crisis into opportunity will prove insufficient."

An important central truth is that the American system of higher education was "never designed to educate most Americans," according to Patrick Callan, president of the National Center for Public Policy in Higher Education. He believes that our restrictive focus leads Americans to measure the success of colleges and universities based on the performance of the institutions themselves, rather than of their students.

Think of the now-infamous media-based rankings of colleges and universities, which serve as almost a biblical template for judging postsecondary "performance". The focus is inherently inward, even when taking into account external factors like the reactions of high school guidance counselors or corporate recruiters. The focus on the institution shifts our attention away from the true design weaknesses in our higher education system as it stands: its failure to provide sufficient access, affordability, and attainment of university education to meet society's future needs.

"The big problem is that high-status institutions tend to compete with each other on academic reputation (which is enhanced by state professors) and bling (luxurious dormitories and fancy sports stadiums) rather than value for money," stated an article in *The Economist* of September 4, 2010. "This luxury model is unlikely to survive what is turning into a prolonged economic downturn. America's universities lost their way badly in the era of easy money. If they do not find it again, they may go the way of GM."

"We're still stuck on having the best higher-education system of the twentieth century, when we're a decade into the twenty-first century," says Callan, whose nonprofit group publishes a biennial report card on the higher-education performance of each state and the country as a whole. By contrast, Callan says, "many of the countries that have made the biggest gains are those that see institutions as a means to an end of achieving social and economic policy."

Despite the clear economic need for America to produce more college graduates—and to do so more quickly—our social and economic policy perspective on the "public value" of higher education is undergoing a major shift that began even before the recent financial crisis. But the value question regarding higher education has been brought into even sharper focus by the Great Recession's continuing effects.

To paraphrase Vice President Dick Cheney's famous dictum about energy conservation, many citizens and politicians are suggesting that support for higher education is now essentially a "private virtue, because those who complete college will have earned their way to sufficient economic privilege to pay (in arrears) for their education even if it was secured by mortgaging their future income with large-scale student loans by borrowing. We have seen the effects of this kind of thinking as state after state cut their direct support of higher education both in real terms and as percentages of their overall budgets. These cuts are down to historically low levels, dipping into the "Two Ski" and "One Ski" tool kits (see Chapter X), while seeming to wait for the Godot named "Normalcy" to return.

We have witnessed the resulting "virtual privatization" of state-supported universities, and the reduced opportunities for entering college that impact not only the economically disadvantaged, but also the middle class. We are drifting by default toward an outcome of far too few higher educational "haves" and far too many "have-nots." Deep down, we know there will be severe consequences both to our standard of living here at home and to our standing in the world.

We know from multiple surveys that the public is caught up in this state of drift. A clear majority believes that a college degree is both necessary for success and that college are becoming unaffordable. Repeated surveys also show the public believes that higher education could do more with less and can add many more students without lowering quality or incessantly raising tuition.

### Market Needs and For-Profit Responses

In business terms, the market is sending universities a message other sectors of the economy have already heard loud and clear. Higher education has enjoyed a unique position among consumer-service businesses, especially those primarily "knowledge-based" and today finds itself in jeopardy. Technology firms, both hardware and software, are continuously challenged to design products and services that deliver more powerful solutions at ever lower costs. Law firms are facing challenges to their time-honored practice of billing by the hour. So are the cost structures of the medical and the related insurance establishments as they squirm under an unrelenting microscope from both public and private perspectives. Yet college tuition pricing has until recently lived the charmed life. The customer has become accustomed—at least up to recently—to annual price increases, well beyond the rate of inflation, for essentially the same (perhaps even less) service and product!

The ambiguities in the public mind about whether higher education remains a "public good"–or is now merely a "private good"–is facing decisive resolution. As direct taxpayer support continues to wane, we essentially force more students to borrow relentlessly against their purported future income to acquire a degree. Access to higher education now comes at an unsustainable price point.

The most significant remaining form of public support for mass college access has devolved to federal direct grants and loans. How ironic that growing amounts of those public, taxpayer funds are finding their way into the fast-growing private for-profit sector, which increased enrollment by 329 percent over the ten years through 2009. That sector which now educates 10 percent of college students (2.6 million) accounts for 25 percent of federal education aid dollars. The American taxpayers fund the lion's share–up to 90 percent in some leading cases–of the for-profit sector's costs and glitzy advertising, not to mention substantial profits.

Enrollment in for-profit higher education is predominantly female; many are single parents, minorities, and first-generation college students. Increasing numbers are active military or veterans. And the for-profit student bodies include large numbers of the minimally employed or recently unemployed. In short, those whose access to higher education is most tenuous are being pulled into the for-profit magnet, and getting in the door through the public subsidy of grants and loans.

Tuition at the for-profit schools, however, is not priced at Wal-Mart levels. For-profit tuition is twice that of the typical four-year public college and an average 500 percent higher than tuition and fees at community colleges. Ironic again, considering that the community-college sector was set up by state and local citizens to provide broad-based access to college, but now is severely constrained in that mission by draconian cutbacks to state and local government budgets. These tuition levels have fostered a student-debt load that now totals $848 billion in outstanding indebtedness. A staggering 96 percent of for-profit students take out loans to pay tuition and fees and school-related expenses. (Compare that to 64 percent of four-year students at state colleges and 72 percent at private nonprofit colleges.) This yields an average $33,000 debt load for those students who have actually graduated from for-profit institutions. Thousands, though, fail to finish and yet take a similar indebtedness burden into a de-leveraging economy. These debt-load figures, according to data developed for Senator Richard Durbin, are nearly $13,000 higher than those accrued by students graduating from public colleges and $5,000 more than those finishing at private nonprofit schools.

Questions are being raised about whether for-profit colleges, with their relatively lower level of instructional expenditures, actually prepare students for "gainful employment" enabling them to pay off their federal loan indebtedness (as detailed in Chapter IV). The latest figures show that the for-profit sector is doing a poor job of delivering on its promise of "attainment," especially for first-time, full-time bachelor's-degree candidates. University of Phoenix, the largest of the for-profit universities, graduates barely 9 percent of this category of students after six years, and only 5 percent of those who study only online.

Senator Durbin asked and answered the obvious question: Why are so many people turning to for-profit colleges for access despite the higher cost and resulting loan burdens? He believes that in addition to the Great Recession, the "failure of public colleges to meet demand is also creating an opportunity for the for-profit schools. Community colleges are being forced to cut classes just when demand is greatest. Public four-year colleges are also laying off staff and turning away students."

There are two additionally important factors in the for-profits' massive enrollment growth. First is the easy access to government loans: for-profit schools have elevated (or devalued) the art of enrolling students with no money upfront. Second is their slick, aggressive and plentiful marketing featuring hard-sell call-center "boiler rooms" (private-sector sales tools that are paid for by public-sector loan largesse). The University of

Phoenix alone spent $6.67 million in a single month (June 2010) just on Google advertising–second only to Apple's ads introducing the iPhone 4!

We know that at critical junctures in times past, the American body politic, when faced with the challenge of access and affordability to higher education, responded with game-changing responses: the Morrill Acts creating the land-grant colleges in the late 1800s; the GI Bill and Truman Commission in the 1940s; and the scientific thrust after the Russians orbited Sputnik in 1957. But 1957 was a long time ago. What has national higher education policy done for us lately? Today, we face another tipping point. And we have added an important "A" word "attainment" in addition to access and affordability. We have now recognized how crucial the attainment of college degrees will be in terms of our national future.

The current "default" solution (simply using massive public subsidies via loans to students to enable them to pay increasingly higher tuition at for-profit schools) in turn funds the for-profits' extraordinary levels of marketing expenditure and returns to shareholders seems to be an inherently wrong-headed, wasteful and risky use of public resources.

Think about it! The US taxpayers, not the for-profit colleges, bear the entire risk of loss on student-loan defaults– more than $800 billion in outstanding loans is higher than even the defaults on subprime mortgages. Taxpayers could wind up with a bill substantially higher than the ultimate cost of the infamous "TARP" rescue of Wall Street.

Clearly our approach to providing access to higher learning needs some fresh thinking. Joni E. Finney, director of the Institute of Research in Higher Education at Penn, borrowed a common high-tech metaphor when she called for a decisive "reset" in higher education. We seem to be in need of what Golden Gate University's president would call a "Blue Ocean" opportunity, and what the Golden Gate University Business School dean would call a "disruptive technology."

Clayton Christenson, the Harvard professor who has done the most to identify this phenomenon and explain its genesis and lifecycle, tells the story of how one such successful business "reinvention" model occurred. It all starts with shifting perspective from a focus on the institution (read: university) to a focus on the customer (read: student).

Christenson asks us to imagine that we are standing on a Mumbai road, watching the large number of motor scooters dashing in and out of the traffic. But it isn't just the number of scooters that is eye-catching. It's that *whole families* are on these scooters! When Ratan Tata surveyed such a scene, he realized that these "scooter families" needed a safer alternative. He knew that a car available in India cost at least five times the price of a scooter. So "access" and "affordability" were clearly obstacles. Tata's insight led him to conceive a powerful consumer "value proposition": he would offer to the "scooter families" an affordable, safe, all-weather transportation alternative. Similar to Henry Ford's assembly line of the early 1900s, there would be the potential to reach millions of people who were not yet part of the car-buying market. Tata also recognized that his Tata Motors' business model could not be used to develop such a product at the needed price.

Tata Motors is India's largest automobile company, with revenues of US $7.2 billion in 2006-2007. With more than 4 million Tata vehicles on the road in India, the firm is the leader in commercial vehicles and the second largest in passenger vehicles. It is also the world's fifth largest medium- and heavy-truck manufacturer and the second largest heavy-bus manufacturer. Tata cars, buses and trucks are also marketed in several countries in Europe, Africa, the Middle East, South Asia, South East Asia and South America. Tata Motors' international footprint includes Tata Daewoo Commercial Vehicle Co. Ltd. in South Korea; Hispano Carrocera, a bus and coach manufacturer of Spain in which the company has a 21 percent stake; a joint venture with Marcopolo, the Brazil-based body-builder of buses and coaches; and a joint venture with Thonburi

Automotive Assembly Plant Company of Thailand to manufacture and market pick-up vehicles in Thailand. Tata Motors has research centers in India, the UK, and in its subsidiary and associate companies in South Korea and Spain.

The new Nano–called "The People's Car" by the company–is designed with a family in mind, comfortably seating four persons. Four doors with high seating position make ingress and egress easy. Yet with a length of 3.1 meters, width of 1.5 meters and height of 1.6 meters, and adequate ground clearance, it is designed to maneuver on busy city roads as well as in rural areas. The People's Car has a rear-wheel drive, with an all-aluminum, two-cylinder, 623 cc, 33 PS, multi-point fuel injection: a two-cylinder gasoline engine. The lean design strategy has helped minimize weight, maximize performance per unit of energy consumed and deliver high fuel efficiency. The Nano's tailpipe emission performance exceeds Indian regulatory requirements, and in terms of overall pollutants, has a lower pollution level than two-wheelers being manufactured in India today.

Tata was able to introduce the new Nano in March 2010 at a slightly higher price (US $2,628) than initially targeted due to higher input costs, factory taxes and new emission rules. Even with an anticipated future price increase at 7.5 percent to affect future intake, the Nano will remain the world's most affordable car. The company received 206,703 orders bookings for the first 100,000 cars manufactured, and the initial deliveries were selected by lottery. Initial production was hampered by violent protests against acquisition of farmland for the first dedicated Nano factory in West Bengal that delayed its opening until June 2010, but another dedicated factory is increasing its annual production to 250,000.

Those who lack affordable access to college in today's America–unless they are willing to assume a crushing future debt load–are like the "scooter families" of Mumbai. For them, we need to design, as did Tata, a truly disruptive technology. Unlike those focusing on more bells and whistles, he conceived a simple "no frills" design at an affordable price.

Thanks to the Tata example and others like it, we now routinely teach in our GGU Business School how a successful disruptive technology starts with a laser-like focus on the "job to be done": solving an important problem or filling an important need for an underserved mass of customers at a price they can afford. This kind of thinking produces what we call the "customer value proposition, which addresses what Christenson has called the four most common barriers that are keeping people from getting a certain job done: cost, access, skill, or time.

Examples of this cited by Christiansen include how Intuit broke the *skills barrier* that kept untrained small-business owners from using a more-complicated accounting package and how MinuteClinic, the drugstore-based basic health-care provider, broke the *time barrier* that kept people from visiting a doctor's office with minor health problems by making nurse practitioners available without prior appointments.

The good news is that a successful entrepreneur of a disruptive technology need not be the "first mover." For-profit higher education clearly has already addressed the *access* and *time barriers* to higher education, particularly for working adults. Their success, achieved with unwitting tax-payer support, addresses the wealth barrier as well through student-loan subsidization. US colleges, with their centuries-old "business model," can take heart from Apple's success with the iPod. As Christenson observed, that company was not the first to market with a digital music player, but it leapfrogged over the initial success of other firms by making *access* to its product even more simple and convenient. The iPod was truly a "game-changer" in terms of the four factors of cost, access, time and skill.

ASU's President Crow, among others, has recognized that new technology (especially the online capacities of higher learning already exploited by the for-profits) can be the great *enabler* **of a new disruptive game-changing business model in publicly funded higher education:** "With the advent of ubiquitous information technologies, traditional institutions no longer enjoy their historic monopoly on higher learning." He predicts that, "During the next ten to fifteen years, developers of new technologies will be leveraging all of their resources and talent to create new learning tools and information-acquisition platforms that make current efforts look like Tinkertoys™."

Employing new technologies holds the promise of squaring the circle around the access/affordability equation in a way that should be within the reach of the public purse. It would at least be more efficient than using taxpayer-subsidized student loans to underserved populations to fund college expenses at high-priced for-profit institutions. And these are institutions that use nearly half the proceeds for marketing and shareholder returns, not academics or student services! But public colleges and universities must first become willing to embrace the possibility of truly disruptive change.

## Adults as the New Traditional Student

The most important word in defining the target audience for our new public-university business model is "adult." We have to first realize that the notion that most people start college right after high school and finish in four years is an urban myth. As a Chronicle Research Services forecast *The College of 2020* concluded, "The idyll of four years away from home–spent living and learning and growing into adulthood–will continue to wane. It will still have a place in higher education, but it will be a smaller piece of the overall picture." This shrinking market is not our "scooter family" target.

Currently, barely a majority of those who start college will finish. This fact creates a vast pool of adults (40 million or so) who already have some college but not enough to earn a degree–a great place to start to define a market that can be well-served by a new "disruptive" college-business model. Through 2016, it is expected that adult learners will represent the fastest growing segment of higher education. The Department of Education has forecast that the eighteen- to twenty-two-year-old college cohort will grow just 7 percent over the next six years; ages twenty-two to twenty-nine will grow 20 percent; and the thirty-plus group will grow 14 percent. As our Generational Barbell chapter shows, all these groups will increasingly be affected by the increasing wants and needs of rising Generation Y.

Adult students have no particular attachment to or identification with the traditional academic calendar. If anything, they appreciate learning in shorter sequential cycles. The traditional semester is falling way to eight- or nine-week terms that are more in synch with today's business calendar than the soil-tilling cycle of nineteenth-century farmers that the traditional academic year was set to accommodate. These adult learners look specifically for courses and program structures that allow them to continue working while in school, and they are quite open to taking courses online.

Among adult graduate students, surveys find only 10 percent prefer the traditional semester. Equally telling, most are strongly motivated toward convenience–including courses offered fully online and hybrid class structures which mix in-person and Internet class sections–with schedules that are asynchronous (i.e. on their own time) regarding *when* and *if* they will attend and participate in "class."

Numerous surveys show that the large and expanding group of adults seeking to complete a bachelor's degree is also the segment most attracted to online courses. The preference for online learning is expected to grow even more as the current K-12 student population, which is intensely engaged with the Internet in their private lives, increasingly experience online learning during their primary and secondary school years.

Both undergraduate and graduate adult learners are increasingly utilitarian in their view of higher education, seeking career-identity in the academic programs they pursue. The same utility-need supports their preference for intensive programs with shorter and tighter delivery schedules that works for them year round.

Today's adults want educational convenience for practical reasons, in terms of balancing work, life and studies. *Tomorrow's* adults, however, will expect "education on demand"–sort of a "curricular Comcast–for the same reasons and even more as a lifestyle preference. The emerging generation (eighteen- to twenty-two years old) will want much the same, although with a somewhat different perspective, particularly in terms of the affordability factor, which will put a different twist on their need for faster paths to degree completion. For the students over twenty-five, *acceleration* is an important option for many who are looking to acquire quickly the skills and certification they need to "move up" in their chosen fields. While for the younger group, it's more a question of accelerating their "move in" to careers, with as low a debt load as possible.

The *Economist* has speculated that both Generation X and Y show signs of desiring to embrace a simpler, less wasteful lifestyle in contrast to the conspicuous consumption of their parents' generation.

For the higher-education segment of "scooter families" the question likely won't be "Can I get a fast car?" so much as "Can I get a car fast?" Affordability will be the largest hurdle for those among this new generation of students so the three-year college degree may be just what the doctor ordered.

Senator Lamar Alexander of Tennessee, a former university president and longtime advocate of students spending less time earning their degrees, put the case well in an October 2009 article in *Newsweek*. "Expanding the three-year option or year-round schedules may be difficult, but it may be more palatable than asking Congress for additional bailout money, asking legislators for more state support, or asking students for even higher tuition payments. Campuses willing to adopt convenient schedules along with more-focused, less-expensive degrees may find that they have a competitive advantage in attracting bright, motivated students."

Three-year degrees need not be "education-lite," but they do require using the entire lunar calendar rather than the antiquated, agrarian-based traditional academic year. Students give up some time off in three-year programs in exchange for reduced all-in cost, particularly in terms of reduced levels of debt they will carry forward.

Senator Alexander highlights the experience of students at Hartwick College in upstate New York, where those who completed a degree in three years saved up to 25 percent in their tuition. Three-year degrees also may produce a dividend in terms of fewer stop-outs and drop outs due to cost considerations because of the lack of major gaps in their learning. Several other colleges and universities in different market segments have introduced or are considering experiments in three-year undergraduate degrees: Maine's Bates College, Judson College in Alabama, Lipscomb University in Tennessee, Ball State in Indiana, the University of Washington, the University of North Carolina Greensboro, and the Universities of Illinois, Indiana and Rhode Island. The three-year concept has even made its way to some of the most traditionally rigorous graduate programs: Penn Law and the Wharton Schools launched an accelerated three-year JD/MBA program in 2009. And two Canadian universities, McMaster and Calgary, will offer MD degrees in three years.

In addition to the obvious efficiency of putting the physical campus to work year-round, the three-year degree concept challenges assumptions long held in American academia that are increasingly out of touch with reality. Most have been protected by entrenched cultures, academic tradition and a sense of "exceptionalism" in American higher education. Senator Alexander, however, sees similarities between such attitudes in higher education and the complacency that led the Big Three in Detroit to their collective doom. Alexander recalled how the prescient industry rebel

George Romney of American Motors early on saw how Detroit's muscle-bound monopoly was "increasingly locked into practices that people knew were destructive."

Edwin Welch, president of the University of Charleston, correctly observed that today most university students do not follow the model embedded in our collective consciousness: the four-year college completion standard. He concludes that "a fast-moving world and the current economic crunch are increasing calls for a three-year college degree." He marveled that while his university had not set up a three-year degree program specifically, one-third of its students managed to complete their bachelor's degree in fewer than four years by using their own initiative to navigate the established curriculum. This naturally evolving result is evidence of considerable pent-up demand for faster degree programs.

More importantly, it shows that by focusing on student learning outcomes, universities are capable of positioning themselves ahead of the demand curve by creating curriculum plans that are flexible enough to accommodate both those students who can benefit from a three-year degree program and those who must take a longer time to finish their baccalaureate because of their work-life circumstances. This kind of flexibility is an essential ingredient if universities are going to become more pro-active in serving the fast-expanding market of working adults. Faster-paced programs, of course, limit the time that working adult students must support their living costs before they can get to the higher-paying job opportunities that can come with degree completion.

Robert Zemsky, chairman of the University of Pennsylvania's Learning Alliance for Education, has also been promoting three-year bachelor's degrees, particularly in terms of combining them with a specialized one- or two-year master's degree. Proposals for no-frills three-year degrees, however, have predictably met with considerable early resistance from traditional quarters in the higher-education establishment.

For example: Carol Geary Schneider, president of the Association of America College and Universities, labeled the three-year degree as a half-baked, deceptively-simple idea reflecting a "new crop of faux reforms that, if adopted, would send us backward." And Alexander C. McCormick, director of Indiana University's National Survey of Student Engagement, initially urged institutions to concentrate on achieving four-year degree completion before thinking about accelerated programs. But these views ignore the evidence that the failure to complete a degree in four, five or even six years is itself due in no small measure to the absence of faster, more flexible programs that reduce the burden on students to finance themselves while they learn.

To the critics of three-year degrees Zemsky responded: "The leadership of the AAC&U has made sustaining the time to degree more important than seeking more timely and efficient means for achieving a college education." His 2009 book, *Making Reform Work: Thre Case for Transforming Higher Education*, champions the three-year degree as a "dislodging" (or as we say "disruptive") event that could break the "logjam that currently holds meaningful reform hostage. As faculty we will have to rethink what we do." Such rethinking, of course, would open the door to using online learning to leverage three-year degree completion.

### The New Model

The design message for our new model is now clear. Those starving for affordable access to a college degree will be served best by a disruptive new "public option"–a no-frills, three-year bachelor's degree delivered via a hybrid of in-person and online courses that "meet" nights, weekends, and even at the work place! There is simply no longer any reason why US taxpayers should continue to "outsource" to the for-profit schools the opportunity to provide this higher education option.

Our new model hits on all four cylinders of the education engine: cost, access, skill and time. It also provides a much-needed pathway to participation by our "scooter families" in this country's economic growth. And it will do so much more efficiently, in terms of public resources, than what the for-profit schools have attempted to do with the benefit of massive taxpayer support.

The question remains: What is the best launching pad for our new model? Starting from scratch is probably not an option; the for-profits captured that flag years ago by recognizing the advantage of *not* having to operate within established academic structures. Since our model envisions a redirection of *public* resources, we need to find the most fertile ground in state-supported academia for planting our seed.

To pick our spot, we must first return for a moment for the work of Professor Christenson and others on the nature of disruptive technologies. The iPod success story discussed earlier in this chapter inspires some level of confidence that innovations can spring from well-established entities. However, the broader evidence to date suggests that relatively few disruptive technologies have emerged from successful companies with firmly embedded business models. This is especially true when the nature of the change can be perceived as going "down market" or as "democratizing" access at the bottom rung of customers.

The "world's low cost car" designed to capture the scooter market in India demanded a whole new business model to accomplish that goal–set apart from the prior successes of Tata Motors. The same will be required in the case of public universities that have been pulled more and more toward "exclusivity of access" in order to enhance their perceived institutional rankings. We need to find the most hospitable setting to renew our historic commitment to providing higher-education opportunity to the broader public at a price that works both for the students and the taxpayers (who are ironically often one and the same).

Christenson relates a disruptive technology success story within a well-established company, Dow-Corning. The company found success with a new disruptive product by setting up a separate business that functioned in a completely different way. "By fundamentally differentiating its low-end and high-end offerings, the company avoided cannibalizing its traditional business even as it found new profits at the low end." Corning was able to maintain separately its core focus on customized solutions for high-margin value-added services and its related existing customer base by designing a new organization that focused totally on customers who needed a *no-frills, low-cost, maximum-efficiency* product.

In the field of higher education there have been some encouraging examples of successful experiments with intensive and online programs at established four-year private nonprofit schools, as well as at major research-oriented state universities. Two traditional bricks-and-mortar schools that have enjoyed success with new Internet-based approaches for serving the adult-learner market are Florida Institute of Technology and Chapman University of California. FIT's online programs are organized in a new academic calendar with six eight-week terms (to facilitate year round learning). The school offers graduate degrees in business and IT, and undergraduate degrees in business and psychology. These programs yielded 4,000 new students in forty states–more than the 3,000 undergrads on FIT's physical campus!

Meanwhile Chapman transformed its University College for adult learners into a *separately-organized* but co-branded Brandman University. All of its students attend online or in hybrid classes at physical locations at twenty-six centers in California and Washington, and the balance on the Internet. A Chapman spokesperson described Brandman's distinct faculty and program offerings as "a big entrepreneurial adventure" that are providing new focus and energy to the university. "For-profit companies have sent a clear message to all of higher education that there is a different way of providing higher education. Students want access to high-quality degrees they can earn while raising families and pursing careers, focused on their needs and convenience."

It is problematic, however, whether the broad spectrum of traditional four-year master's and doctoral institutions is as ready as Dow-Corning's management (or Chapman's and FIT's) to step aside from their entrenched focus on exclusivity rankings to embrace a entirely new approach to a market they all but abandoned a long time ago.

The most promising launch site for a new no-frills, three-year degree, especially employing the latest Internet technology, may well be "America's College"–the community college sector. Until recently this sector has been generally constrained from offering full baccalaureate degrees, but it stands able and willing to do so. Seventeen states now allow community colleges to offer undergraduate degree programs; Florida community colleges which offer more than 100 full undergraduate degrees!

To start with, community colleges already have an outsized role in online education. While these colleges collectively teach about 37 percent of higher education students,

More than half of all online students are enrolled by community colleges, according to research by the Sloan Consortium. Sloan determined that this pattern of associate-level colleges claiming a large share of online enrollments has shown considerable consistency during the first decade of the twenty-first century. Moreover, community colleges already are familiar with serving adult students; in California, for example, they constitute the clear majority. And community colleges already have in place the kind of cost structure that could effectively compete with for-profit universities, should they choose to make convenient three-year degrees available to the working-adult "customers"–a segment that the for-profits now think they own.

The added cost of mounting the upper-division courses needed for baccalaureate degree completion could well be accommodated within the

500 percent spread between for-profit and community college tuition rates! A price point could be set that would be less than tuition at traditional four-year state-supported universities and well below that charged by private nonprofit colleges. Such a price point would yield an attractive alternative for our higher education "scooter families." Moreover, default rates are far lower at community colleges than at for-profits like University of Phoenix; and graduates of community colleges needed to borrow much less to finish their degrees, so leave school with considerably less debt.

Based on all the evidence, it is abundantly clear that establishing a new, no-frills, three-year hybrid degree model in the distinctly American community college setting will generate a much better relative return for taxpayer investment in higher education than the for-profits are now providing with federal student loan money–with much less risk of loss due to loan defaults.

Community colleges are already the institutions that serve the majority of students in underrepresented populations. They are the best-positioned to follow the Dow Corning example and successfully generate a new disruptive technology that will serve nontraditional student customers who will be the backbone of our future economic development–provided they find a way to complete their degrees.

We know that without having multiple evening, hybrid, and online courses in place, public universities will not attract or increase access for these students–and the community colleges are already "there" in terms of delivering those types of courses. Community colleges were originally conceived to be an innovative "disruption" to academic complacency, and they can be called to respond yet again in our current crisis.

What are the most serious obstacles to success of our three-year, no-frills, hybrid-format community-college-based new university? Beyond just the "traditional" resistance to community colleges offering bachelor's degrees (which we to propose to "disrupt", head-on), the first important barrier comes down to institutional ignorance of the true economics of providing a college education. Except for the for-profits, many colleges continue to operate in a vacuum in terms of sophisticated information about mission-related accounting and performance metrics. Colleges need better data with respect to programmatic market share, competitive position, cost allocations and gross margin calculations by program, retention rates, and learning outcomes. In short, many universities operate with only a primitive picture of the productivity of their offerings, and thus leave their program management choices to "educated" guesses.

Many colleges and universities tend to behave as if riding the San Francisco BART train. That is, they shy away from touching the electrified third rail with real knowledge of their basic economics rather than well-worn assumptions. But touch the third rail they must. And we have outlined a number of creative steps how to do that in our "Barefoot Skiing" chapter.

Fortunately, many US foundations are channeling their support toward ways that universities can do more with less. The Sloan Foundation has made generous grants to encourage sophisticated development of online courses and delivery techniques. The Lumina Foundation's "Making Opportunity Affordable" initiative encourages and rewards institutions that focus on student completion, program quality and expanded and strengthened nontraditional, low-cost educational options.

A Lumina grant to Arizona, one of the states worst hit by the housing crisis and Great Recession, was structured to foster "no-frills" offerings including through existing community college partnerships with four-year institutions and to redesign financial aid models to provide more incentives for students to complete their education. Similar grants to Montana, Ohio, Maryland, Indiana, Tennessee and Texas focus on redesigning course structures, aid formulas, and productivity measures to foster degree completion. In several cases, these grants also focus on community colleges as the essential "hub" in accomplishing this re-democratization of higher education. Lumina has clearly touched the third rail by focusing on *productivity* in urging 23 million more college graduates in the next fifteen years: "Our higher education systems and institutions must increase their productivity and capacity to meet the growing demand, in fact, they will have to develop alternative delivery systems. . .that incorporate new technologies, competency-based approaches, and other innovations."

In this connection, the draft *Report of the Advisory Committee on Higher Education Cost Efficiencies* to the Texas Higher Education Coordinating Board recommended four specific approaches to enhance productivity for consideration by campus leaders. First, creating continuous improvement councils on campus to make sure that productivity improvement remains a priority. Second, requiring that 10 percent of degree credits be attained through means not involving on-campus classroom activity (including online). Third, by improving credit hours produced per faculty member by 10 percent; and, finally, by requiring students to have a degree plan by the end of the freshman year and to meet with an advisor prior to enrolling in a course not included in the plan.

Similar innovations in educational productivity are already occurring at the more "granular" class level in ways that suggest enormous potential for a new three-year degree model.

Robert Olin, dean of arts and sciences at the University of Alabama, has championed a math lab that has revolutionized entry-level classes. Students no longer spend three or four hours a week listening to lectures and doing homework. The new classes utilize only forty minutes of lecture and then practice on specially programmed computers in the math lab where tutors answer questions. It costs about one-third less than a traditional lecture class and students score higher on the final exam than their counterparts in more traditional classes. Several other universities, including the University of Massachusetts, Amherst and the State University of New York system, are conducting similar course redesigns.

A number of other steps toward more efficiency for both students and schools alike can be readily incorporated into our new model, particularly in terms of serving working adults. Much good work on this front has been done by the Counsel on Adult and Experiential Learning (CAEL). Several ideas originally presented to the Commission on the Future of Higher Education by CAEL's president, Pamela Tate, are reflected (with enthusiasm) in the following paragraphs.

Credit for "experiential" prior learning, including on-the-job training, military experience, and even certain types of volunteer work is increasingly acknowledged in many universities. Appraisal of such experience could be developed to a level of sophistication where students can submit portfolios framed in a manner analogous to the submissions that faculty members make to justify their own re-appointments and advancement in rank.

Considerable work can be done to redesign student-aid formulas to support accelerated-degree programs by moving them away from designs that reflect the traditional academic year. Tax-advantaged lifelong-learning accounts are another mechanism that could be initiated along the lines of flexible spending; and medical and childcare reimbursement structures already existing under the federal tax code. Federal tax credits, which now primarily benefit families who claim them on behalf of their dependents, could be expanded to provide more support for working adults themselves.

Many states are encouraging colleges within their own systems to develop better in-house transfer of credits to make transition from two-year to baccalaureate programs much more seamless and understandable.

Funding formulas sometimes penalize institutions with large numbers of part-time students because they concentrate resources based on "full-time equivalence formulas." These could be refocused on raw student headcount, which would lead administrators to be much more hospitable toward adult learners.

Accreditors can provide more flexibility with respect to offering on-site learning programs at corporate and government offices, especially at the graduate level. This is important so that universities that undertake course delivery innovations would not have to go through a lengthy approval process associated with creating new physical teaching "sites"–a process that was designed for a completely different "distance-education" era. Many of these corporate programs are already delivered in significant measure online and do not require the kind of physical asset scrutiny involved when a university sets up a traditional, open-to-the-public mini-campus away from its home base.

Some accreditation rules seem curiously strict and rigid–especially when, in unbelievable contrast–for-profit universities have been allowed by the same accreditors to simply *purchase* the accreditation of an existing institution, and change its character completely with no review. "Accreditation has become like a taxi medallion, available for bidding on the open market," observed Kevin Carey, policy director of Education Sector, a Washington, DC think tank.

Bearing in mind our focus on serving working adults more efficiently, we should also be concerned that workers in many states lose their unemployment benefits when they enroll in college. But, at the same time, if they become unemployed, their prior year's earnings may disqualify them for Pell Grants. Obviously these factors discourage unemployed workers from going back to school and should be reconsidered at both the state and federal levels. And states can partner with businesses in the technology field in developing social media vehicles that would allow community colleges to maintain a virtual "touch" with the increasing number of working-adult students they serve online.

Traditional-age students already are more likely to use social networking tools to communicate with other students, instructors and college staff on an almost 24/7 basis. We can stimulate experiments in setting up virtual interest groups online where working-adult students can participate in virtual extracurricular activities. Our future "Joe" or "Jane College" may have an Avatar as a roommate!

As we look ahead to realize our new model of a public-serving university, we close with a learned glimpse from the past.

One of the foremost trend-spotters of our era, Daniel Yankelovich, several years ago looked ahead as to where he thought higher education would be in 2015. He predicted that the old pattern of attending college from age eighteen to twenty-two "was evaporating." He suggested that colleges and universities should work more closely with employers to generate more efforts to integrate higher education, work to recognize this new lifecycle pattern, and make education much more practical and career-focused.

He also focused on the group aged fifty-five to seventy-five in terms what he saw as a "second-life" stage. Given that retirement age no longer means total withdrawal from other forms of life fulfillment, he believed there was great potential and that higher education should respond to that call. As many older Americans seek to build new bridges to life opportunities, nostalgia for college years can draw their focus "back to campus." But the typical curriculum (both undergraduate and graduate) is a poor fit for their needs.

Another great opportunity for universities for experimentation and innovation and disruptive technology modeling is clearly emerging with this age group. Yankelovich concluded that colleges would have a strong economic incentive to be more creative in matching the needs of older adults with more suitable learning materials and more convenient timetables. As we now know, older adults even show themselves open to learning in online and hybrid settings. This particular opportunity suggests that embracing our new model of flexible higher learning could provide colleges with an *economic double-play*. Making access, affordability and attainment available are important not only to the *emerging* generations that are the future of our workforce, but also to the *older* generation which itself is looking for new ways to serve. Here again, the benefit to society is potentially enormous because we know that our retirement systems will undergo tremendous strain as the baby boomers continue to age gracefully but not always gainfully. Offering them a flexible opportunity to continue to contribute to our economic and social well-being is a highly attractive social "value proposition."

Our disruptive, double-play solution is thus a boon for both ends of the Generational Barbell and will allow us to deflect the California Bellwether, take advantage of powerful online tools, reverse the drift toward expensive dependency on Taxpayer U, and to rediscover and even reinvent America's College.

To accomplish our goal of ending Graduation Gridlock for all higher education's generations–at a price taxpayers can feel good about paying– we must understand that the Riptide of the Great Recession is real, and stop Waiting for Godot. We must be aware of the competition from Over There, and relieve the Big Squeeze on the Alma Mater by thinking outside the established box to achieve all three desired outcomes: access, affordability, and *attainment* of degrees.

To succeed, we will need to Ski Barefoot, touch the Third Rail, and fully embrace our no frills, three-year "public option."

RIPTIDE indeed!

# HEAT
## Higher Education Awareness
## Test Answer Sheet

1.  Forty percent of Americans over age twenty-five have a college degree. (F)
2.  Most college students are under age twenty-two. (F)
3.  Online college courses typically cost less than in-person courses. (F)
4.  For-profit universities are allowed to receive up to 90 percent of their tuition revenue in the form of federal education loans and grants. (T)
5.  Endowments at private schools were largely insulated from the effects of the Great Recession by conservative invest ment policies. (F)
6.  Since the onset of the Great Recession, state colleges and universities have generally held tuition increases below the rate of inflation. (F)
7.  Despite the increase of for-profit and online universities, most US college students still attend school in the traditional four-year residential setting. (F)
8.  The average "discount rate" (the amount private colleges actually charge students) is 10 percent less than the sticker price. (F)
9.  The World Economic Forum's 2010 Global Competitive ness Report lists America as among the top in all twelve categories. (F)
10. China uses more energy than the US. (T)
11. In terms of college degrees, younger Americans (age twenty-five to thirty-four) have made significant gains in the

past thirty years. (F)

12. CalPERS, the largest public employee retirement system in the nation, once predicted the Dow Jones Industrial Average would be 25,000 by 2009. (T)

13. "iGen" is a major breakthrough in computer technology. (F)

14. Community colleges began by adding grades 13 and 14 to high school. (T)

15. University presidents supported the start of community colleges. (T)

16. Vice President Joe Biden's wife Jill is a community college instructor. (T)

17. Most economists believe state revenues will be back to normal by 2012. (F)

18. High education spent more than $90 billion on new construction between 2002 and 2008. (T)

19. Consumer spending drives 70 percent of our economy. (F)

20. Traditional college students (ages 18 to 22) comprise 60 percent of today's college students. (F)

21. California is the only state in the nation to require a two-thirds vote to pass both the state budget and a statewide tax increase. (F) (True until 2010)

22. Canada is the world leader in the higher education completion rate. (T)

23. Forty-five of every 100 students who start college today will not earn a bachelor's degree. (T)

24. The federal government keeps six year records on four year college degrees. (T)

25. Current outstanding federal government student loan debt is higher than the entire TARP "bailout" or the whole Obama Stimulus Package. (T)

# RIPTIDE BIBLIOGRAPHY

Tom Abate, "Jobless Rate Falls as Many Giving Up," *San Francisco Chronicle*, July 3, 2010.

Associated Press, "Perdue Says NC Colleges Must Rely on Private Gifts," Associated Press via NBC17, November 30, 2010, www2.nbc17.com/news/2010/nov/30/perdue-says-nc-colleges-must-rely-private-gifts-ar-577736/.

Michael Berland, "How the Economic Crisis Changed Us," *Parade*, (November 1, 2009).

Anthony Carnevale, Nicole Smith and Jeff Strohl, *Help Wanted: Projections of Jobs and Education Requirements through 2018*, Georgetown University, http://cew.georgetown.edu/jobs2018/

Dennis Caucheon, "Tax Bills in 2009 at Lowest Level since 1950," *USA Today*, May 11, 2010.

Michael Crowley, "The Economy is Back; The Economy Stinks," *TIME*, July 28, 2010.

Paul Davidson, "Expect Lots of Layoffs at Sate, Local Levels.," *USA Today*, July 6, 2010.

Delta Project, *Trends in College Spending 1998-2008*, July 2010, http://www.deltacostproject.org/resources/pdf/Trends-in-College-Spending-98-08.pdf

Editorial, "Census: Income fell sharply last year," *USA Today*, April 10, 2010).

Roger W. Ferguson Jr., *A New Normal for Higher Education* (TIAA-CREF, January 4, 2009).

Scott Jaschik, "Historic Declines," *Inside Higher Education*, January 18, 2010, http://www.insidehighered.com/news/2010/01/18/grapevine.

Brian Kelly, "Colleges in the Cross Hairs," editor's note, *US News & World Report*, September 2009.

Barbara Kiviat, "How to Create a Job," *TIME*, March 29, 2010.

Doug Lederman, "Slipping Further Off the Pedestal," *Inside Higher Education*, February 17, 2010, http://www.insidehighered.com/news/2010/02/17/squeeze.

Kathleen Megan, "CSUS Trustee Recind 'Pay Equity' Raises," *Hartford Courant,* July 27, 2010.

Cecilia Rouse, *Higher Ed and the Great Recession* (Council of Economic Advisers, March 4, 2010).

Richard Wolf, "Social Security Collectors Up 19%," *USA Today,* October 14, 2009; and "Don't Expect Additional Stimulus Bills from Feds," *USA Today*, December 8, 2008.

Mark Zandi, *From the Great Recession to Economic Recovery to Expansion* (Moody's Analytics, December 2010), http://www.moodys.com.

Mortimer Zuckerman, "Time to Act on a Bleak Fiscal Future," *US News & World Report*, April 2010.

## THE BIG SQUEEZE ON ALMA MATER BIBLIOGRAPHY

Tom Abate, "State education cuts hurt economy, report says," *San Francisco Chronicle*, May 6, 2010, http://articles.sfgate.com/2010-05-06/business/20887809_1_bay-area-regional-economy-global-headquarters.

Brittany Anas,. "CU regents indicate they'll OK 9 percent tuition hike, set March 29 vote," *Boulder Daily Camera*, March 10, 2010, http://www.dailycamera.com/cu-news/ci_14647959.

Associated Press and Star-Bulletin Staff, "UH moves to cut faculty salaries 6.7 percent," *Honolulu Star-Bulletin*, December 28, 2009.

Associated Press, "Perdue Says NC Colleges Must Rely on Private Gifts," Associated Press via NBC17, November 30, 2010, www2.nbc17.com/news/2010/nov/30/perdue-says-nc-colleges-must-rely-private-gifts-ar-577736/.

Nanette Asimov, "UC to lend state millions to kick-start construction," *San Francisco Chronicle,* August 6, 2009, D1&6.

Nanette Asimov, "S.F. City College cancels summer session," *San Francisco Chronicle*, February 4, 2010, A-1, http://articles.sfgate.com/2010-02-04/news/17847292_1_community-college-league-summer-session-classes-than-last-year.

Andrew Bary, "The Big Squeeze," *Barron's*, June 29, 2009.

Doug Blackburn, "FSU layoffs of tenured faculty cause a stir," *Tallahassee Democrat*, February 19, 2010.

Goldie Blumenstyk, "Colleges Undermine Their Value When They Put Tuition 'On Sale,'" *Chronicle of Higher Education*, May 29, 2009, A24; and "In Time of Uncertainty, Colleges Hold Fast to Status Quo," *Chronicle of Higher Education*, October 30, 2009, A1 & 14-16; and "Negative Credit Ratings Reflect Rising Financial Strain on Small Colleges," *Chronicle of Higher Education*, July 30, 2010, A15.

Kelley Bouchard, "Community colleges freeze tuition again," *Portland Press Herald*, April 14, 2010, http://www.pressherald.com/news/Community-colleges-freeze-tuition-again.html.

Bill Bush, "OSU to raise tuition 7 percent by fall," *Columbus Dispatch*,

May 15, 2010, http://www.dispatch.com/live/content/local_news/stories/2010/05/15/osu-to-raise-tuition-7-percent-by-fall.html.

Albert Carnesale, "The Private-Public Gap in Higher Education," *Chronicle of Higher Education*, January 6, 2006, B20.

"College enrollment: Boom times," *Economist*, November 14, 2009.

Jennifer Epstein, "Questioning Endowment Losses," *Inside Higher Ed*, May 21, 2010, http://www.insidehighered.com/news/2010/05/21/endowments

Paul Fain, "Less for More," *New York Times Education Life*, November 1, 2009, pp. 20-23.

Andrea Fuller, "Led by North Dakota, Some States Shield Higher Education from Cutbacks," *Chronicle of Higher Education*, March 26, 2010, A27-28.

Roger Goodman, *Impact of the Credit Crisis and A Weaker Economy on US Higher Education* (Moody's Investors Service, Report Number 111958, October 2008).

Roger Goodman, Outlook *Update: Immediate Pressures on US Higher Education are Easing* (Moody's Investors Service, Report Number 120018, September 2009).

Darryl G Greer and Michael W. Klein, "Fixing the Broken Financing Model," *Inside Higher Ed*, October 4, 2010, http://www.insidehighered.com/views/2010/10/04/greer.

Ralph K.M. Haurwitz, "Texas colleges counting economic blessings–for now," *Austin American-Statesman,* December 7, 2009, http://www.statesman.com/news/content/news/stories/local/2009/12/07/1207colleges.html

Sara Hebel, "State Cuts are Pushing Public Colleges into Peril,"

*Chronicle of Higher Education*, March 19, 2010, A1&18-22.

Daniel J. Hurley, *Considerations for State Colleges and Universities in a Post-Recession America* (American Association of State Colleges and Universities, November 2009).

Tracy Jan, "Harvard to offer first retirement plan for professors," *Boston Globe*, December 3, 2009,http://www.boston.com/news/ education/higher/articles/2009/12/03/ harvard_to_offer_first_retirement_plan_for_professors/; and "Faculty cuts at Brandeis proposed," Boston Globe, February 23, 2010, http:// www.boston.com/news/education/higher/articles/2010/02/23/ faculty_cuts_at_brandeis_proposed/.

Scott Jaschik, "Waiting for Recovery," *Inside Higher Ed*, May 4, 2010, http://www.insidehighered.com/news/2010/05/04/aera.

Karin Kapsidelis, "VCU raises tuition by 24 percent," *Richmond Times-Dispatch*, April 30, 2010, http://www2.timesdispatch.com/ news/2010/apr/30/vcuu30_20100429-221804-ar-159732/.

Kevin Kiley, "Results of State Referenda Related to Higher Education," *Chronicle of Higher Education,* November 12, 2010, A19.

Christopher D. Kirkpatrick, "Tuition skyrockets as colleges pay big salaries; maximum boosts set at UT, BGSU," *Toledo Blade,* May 16, 2010, http://www.toledoblade.com/apps/pbcs.dll/article?AID=/ 20100516/NEWS16/100519858

Lisa M. Krieger, "In an economic downturn, even Stanford University's fundraisers have to cut back," *San Jose Mercury News*, May 11, 2009.

Whitney Kvasager, *Richest Endowments Face Collective $38B Loss* (FundFire, June 17, 2009, www.fundfire.com).

Doug Lederman, "Slight Rebound for Endowments," *Inside Higher*

*Ed*, December 10, 2009, http://www.insidehighereducation.com/news/2009/12/10/endow.

Kate Linebaugh, "Michigan's Broken 'Promise,'" *Wall Street Journal*, November 23, 2009, http://online.wsj.com/article/NA_WSJ_PUB:SB125893723996459927.html.

Tim Martin, "Possible Budget Cuts Could Raise Mich. Tuition," Associated Press, March 16, 2010, http://www.huffingtonpost.com/2010/03/17/possible-budget-cuts-coul_n_502542.html

Kathryn Masterson, "Private Giving to Colleges Dropped Sharply in 2009," *Chronicle of Higher Education*, February 12, 2010, A24-25.

M. McDonald, "Paying the Price for Following Yale," *Bloomberg Businessweek*, September 30, 2010.

John C. Nelson and Roger Goodman, *US Colleges and Universities Rating Roadmap: Focus on Special Risks During Recession and Credit Crisis* (Moody's Investors Service, Report Number 117008., April 2009).

Christopher Newfield and Mark G. Yudof, "Commentary: Two Perspectives on the Crisis in California," *Chronicle of Higher Education*, October 9, 2009, A30-32.

An Le Nguyen, "Study: endowment hit harder than average," *Stanford Daily*, February 4, 2010.

Yalman Onaran, "Colleges Flunk Economics Test as Harvard Model Destroys Budgets," *Bloomberg*, May 1, 2009, http://www.bloomberg.com/apps/news?pid=newsarchive&sid=aoglHAxZffTI

Richard C. Paddock, "Hard times at UC, Cal State," *Contra Costa Times*, October 8, 2007, A1&17.

Laurel Rosenhall, "CSU board votes to hike tuition," *Sacramento Bee*,

November 10, 2010, http://www.fresnobee.com/2010/11/10/2154250/
csu-board-votes-to-hike-tuition.html.

Jack Stripling, "Fading Stimulus Saved Colleges," *Inside Higher Ed*,
February 1, 2010, http://www.insidehighered.com/news/2010/02/11/
sheeo; and "Slashing Prices," *Inside Higher Ed,* March 31, 2010,
http://www.insidehighered.com/news/2010/03/31/discounting.

Beckie Supiano, "As Tough Times Persist, Colleges Must Live with
Last Year's Decisions," *Chronicle of Higher Education*, , February
12, 2010, A30.

Chavon Sutton, "Public college tuitions spike 15%, even 30%,"
*CNNMoney*, February 24, 2010, http://money.cnn.com/2010/02/24/
news/economy/public_tuition_soars/.

William C. Symonds, "Should Public Universities Behave Like Private
Colleges?" *BusinessWeek,* November 15, 2004, 97-100.

Dorie Turner, "Ga. Regents approve up to 16 percent tuition hike,"
*BusinessWeek*, May 11, 2010, http://www.businessweek.com/ap/
financialnews/D9FKRUP81.htm

Wayne Washington, "State considers cutting even more from spending
on colleges and universities," *Island Packet*, November 30, 2009,
http://www.islandpacket.com/2009/11/30/1052244/state-considers-
cutting-even-more.html

Robin Wilson (with additional reporting by Elyse Ashburn, Scott
Carlson, Audrey Williams June, Eric Kelderman, Kathryn Masterson,
and Beckie Supiano), "As Credit Crisis Chills Campuses, Worries
Mount," *Chronicle of Higher Education*, October 10, 2008, A1&17-
18.

Austin Wright, "Cash-Strapped Public Colleges Plan for Likely Decline
in Lucrative Out-of-State Enrollments," *Chronicle of Higher Education*, September 4, 2009, A38-39.

# GRADUATION GRIDLOCK BIBLIOGRAPHY

Kurt Badenhausen and Lesley Kump, "Part-Time Fever," *Forbes*, September 5, 2005, 148-152.

Sandra Block, "In a recession, is college worth it? Fear of debt changes plans," *USA Today*, August 31, 2009, http://www.usatoday.com/money/perfi/college/2009-08-30-college-costs-recession_N.htm.

John Bound, Michael Lovenheim and Sarah Turner, *Why have college completion rates declined? An analysis of changing student preparation and collegiate resources (working paper)* (NBER Working Paper Series, working paper #15566).

Scott Carlson, Kathryn Masterson and Jeffrey Brainard, "The $50K Club: 58 Private Colleges Pass a Pricing Milestone," *Chronicle of Higher Education*, November 6, 2009,. A1&22-23.

Anthony P. Carnevale, "Discounting Education's Value," *Chronicle of Higher Education*, September 22,2006, B6-9; and "Hitting the Books Still Pays Off," *BusinessWeek*, July 17, 2006.

Dennis Cauchon, "Incomes of young in 8-year nose dive," *USA Today*, September 18, 2009.

Joseph Marr Cronin and Howard E. Horton, "Will Higher Education be the Next Bubble to Burst?" *Chronicle of Higher Education*, Commentary, May 22, 2009, http://chronicle.com/article/Will-Higher-Education-Be-the/44400

John Immerwahr and Jean Johnson (with Amber Ott and Jonathan Rochkind), *Squeeze Play 2010: Continued Public Anxiety on Cost, Harsher Judgements on How Colleges are Run*, (Public Agenda, joint project of the National Center for Public Policy and Public Agenda, 2010, http://www.publicagenda.org/pages/squeeze-play-2010).

Jean Johnson and Jon Rochkind (with Amber N. Ott and Samantha DuPont), *With Their Whole Lives Ahead of Them*, (Public Agenda, prepared for the Bill and Melinda Gates Foundation. December 2009, http://www.publicagenda.org/theirwholelivesaheadofthem).

Mike Konczal, "Student Loans are the New Indentured Servitude," *Atlantic,* October 12, 2009, http://www.theatlantic.com/business/ archive/2009/10/student-loans-are-the-new-indentured-servitude/ 28235/.

Doug Lederman, "Economy Sinks, Default Rates Rise," *Inside Higher Ed,* September 15, 2009, http://www.insidehighered.com/news/2009/ 09/15/default.

Noam N. Levey, "17.3% of US spending in '09 went to medical, report says," *Chicago Tribune*, February 4, 2010.

Tamar Lewin, "Report Finds Low Graduation Rates at For-Profit Colleges," *New York Times*, November 23, 2010, http:// www.nytimes.com/2010/11/24/education/24colleges.html.

David Moltz, "Falling Education Attainment," *Inside Higher Ed,* May 10, 2010, http://www.insidehighered.com/news/2010/05/10/demographics.

Sarah O'Connor, "Concerns grow for new lost generation," *Financial Times*, November 25, 2009.

Kimberly Palmer, "The Day the Spending Stopped: A new frugality could remake the US economy- and American life," *US News & World Report*, August 2008.

Greg Perfetto, *The End of Higher Education Enrollment as We Know It* (Admissions Lab, White Paper No. 1., 2010, http:// www.admissionslab.com/Education/WhitePapers.aspx).

L. Tamar, "Once a Leader, US Lags in College Degrees, Report

Finds," *New York Times*, July 23, 2010, http://www.nytimes.com/2010/07/23/education/23college.html?_r; and "Average College Debt Rose to $24,000 in 2009, Report Finds," *New York Times*, October 22, 2010, http://www.universitybusiness.com/newssummary.aspx.

"Solving the College Crisis," *US News & World Report*, September 2009.

Emmeline Zhao, "Fewer Low-Income Students Going to College Report Finds," *New York Times*, October 25, 2010, www.universitybusiness.com/newssummary.aspx?news=yes&postid.


ONLINE GAINS TRACTION BIBLIOGRAPHY

Nanette Asimov, "UC regents endorse test of online instruction," *San Francisco Chronicle*. July 15, 2010, http://articles.sfgate.com/2010-07-15/bay-area/21983954_1_regent-sherry-lansing-regent-bonnie-reiss-uc-commission.

Paul Basken and Libby Nelson, "Despite Budget Austerity, Obama Proposes Increases for Education and Research," *Chronicle of Higher Education*, February 12, 2010, A27-29.

Marc Beja, "Online Campus Could Solve Many of U. of California Problems, a Dean Says," *Chronicle of Higher Education*, July 22, 2009, http://chronicle.com/article/Online-Campus-Could-Solve-Many/47432/.

Goldie Blumenstyk, "Touro College Tests New Waters with Proposed Sale of Online Unit," *Chronicle of Higher Education,* September 26, 2006, A42.

Goldie Blumenstyk, "Q&A: Tough Questions for a Career-College Leader," *Chronicle of Higher Education*, February 12, 2010, A23.

Eric Bradner, "Indiana launches online university," *Evansville Courier*

& *Press*, June 12, 2010, http://www.courierpress.com/news/2010/jun/12/indiana-launchesonlineuniversity/.

Margaret Brooks, "The Excellent Inevitability of Online Courses," *Chronicle of Higher Education*, May 29, 2009, http://chronicle.com/article/The-Excellent-Inevitability-of/44251/.

David R. Butcher, "Online Degrees Viewed More Favorably," *ThomasNet News: Industry Market Trends*, October 13, 2009, http://news.thomasnet.com/IMT/archives/2009/10/online-college-degrees-viewed-more-favorably-according-to-reports-still-some-skepticism.html.

Dan Carnevale, "Rule Change May Spark Online Boom for Colleges," *Chronicle of Higher Education*, February 3, 2006, http://chronicle.com/article/Rule-Change-May-Spark-Online/14648.

*Competing in Online Higher Education: Positioning and Differentiation Strategies*, (Eduventures, Inc., Learning Collaborative for Higher Education, February 2006).

"Daniels announces opportunity to increase access to higher education," *IN.gov.*, June 11, 2010, http://www.in.gov/portal/news_events/54822.htm.

"Data Points: Growth in For-Profit Colleges' Proportion of Students and Federal Aid," *Chronicle of Higher Education,* July 2, 2010.

Trip Gabriel, "Learning in Dorm, because Class Is on the Web," *New York Times*, November 4, 2010, http://www.nytimes.com/2010/11/05/us/05college.html.

Daniel Golden, "G.I. Bill of Goods," *Bloomberg BusinessWeek*, January 11, 2010.

Brenda Harms, *Stamats 2008 Adult StudentsTALK™ Study* (Stamats, Inc., PowerPoint Presentation, October 8, 2009).

Josh Keller and Marc Parry, "U. of California Considers Online Classes, or Even Degrees," *Chronicle of Higher Education*, May 14, 2010, A1&11-12.

Kathleen Kingsbury, "Go Western, Young Man," *TIME*, November 13, 2008, http://www.time.com/time/magazine/article/ 0,9171,1858876,00.html.

Steve Kolowich, *Inside Higher Ed*: "IT Budgets Take a Hit," November 4, 2009, http://www.insidehighered.com/news/2009/11/04/ educause; "Student Clubs, Virtually," March 10, 2010, http:// www.insidehighered.com/news/2010/03/10/clubs; "Seed of Doubt," June 22, 2010, http://www.insidehighered.com/news/2010/06/22/ online; "Buying Local, Online," July 23, 2010, http:// www.insidehighered.com/news/2010/07/23/online; "California Dreamer," August 3, 2010, http://www.insidehighered.com/news/2010/ 08/03/california; "Internal Barriers to Online Expansion," November 12, 2010, http://www.insidehighered.com/news/2010/11/12/online; and "Speeding toward a Slowdown?" November 16, 2010, http:// www.insidehighered.com/news/focus/technology/online_learning/survey.

Carol Lloyd, "Online education comes into its own," *San Francisco Chronicle*, August 2, 2009, http://articles.sfgate.com/2009-08-02/ living/17175552_1_online-education-sloan-consortium-traditional-universities.

Mary Beth Marklein, "Probe finds fraud and deception at for-profit colleges," *USA Today*, August 4, 2010, D5; and "'Tight' rules sought for for-profit schools," *USA Today*, August 5, 2010,).

David Nagel,. "Most College Students to Take Classes Online by 2014," *Campus Technology*, October 28, 2009, http:// campustechnology.com/Articles/2009/10/28/Most-College-Students-To-Take-Classes-Online-by-2014.aspx?Page=1.

Bob Sevier, "How Engaged are Online Students?" *Stamats, Inc. QuickTakes Newsletter*, vol. 13, no. 2, January 28, 2010.

Jack Stripling, "The Rise of 'Edupunk,'" *Inside Higher Ed*, November 5, 2010, http://www.insidehighered.com/news/2010/11/05/cref.

Beckie Supiano, ,). "As Tough Times Persist, Colleges Must Live with Last Year's Decisions," *Chronicle of Higher Education*, February 12, 2010, A30.

Jeffrey A. Trachtenberg, "Textbooks Offered for iPod, iPhones," *Wall Street Journal*, August 10, 2009.

Martin Van Der Werf and Grant Sabatier, *The College of 2020: Students* (Chronicle Research Services, June 2009.

Robin Wilson, "For-Profit Colleges Change Higher Education's Landscape," *Chronicle of Higher Education*, February 12, 2010, A1&16-19.

Iza Wojciechowska, "Continuing Debate Over Online Education," *Inside Higher Ed*, July 16, 2010, http://www.insidehighered.com/news/2010/07/16/online.

## TAXPAYER U BIBLIOGRAPHY

*Fiscal 2009 Fourth Quarter and Year End Results* (Apollo Group, Inc. Reports; Business Wire, October 27, 2009).

Associated Press, "For-profit colleges see higher rate of loan defaults," December 14, 2009. .

Gary A. Berg, "Reform Higher Education with Capitalism?" *Change*, May/June 2005.

Dan Berrett, "Hirings Rocket at For-Profits," *Inside Higher Ed*, November 4, 2010, http://www.insidehighered.com/news/2010/11/04/nces.

Joan Berkes, "Final Program Integrity Rules: Gainful Employment," *News from NASFAA,* November 5, 2010, http://www.nasfaa.org/publications/2010/rnfinalrulesgainfulemployment110510.html.

Goldie Blumenstyk, *Chronicle of Higher Education:* "Why For-Profit Colleges are Like Health Clubs," May 5, 2006, A35-36; "The Chronicle Index of For-Profit Higher Education," November 9, 2007, A27; "Documentary on For-Profit Colleges Hits Some Targets and Some Nerves,". May 14, 2010, A16-17; "Business Is Up in Keeping Default Rates Down," July 11, 2010, http://chronicle.com/article/Business-Is-Up-in-Keeping/66226/; and "New Federal Rule Threatens Practices and Revenue at For-Profit Colleges," October 22, 2010, http://chronicle.com/article/Academic-Credit-New-Federal/124972/.

Eryn Brown, "Can For-Profit Schools Pass an Ethics Test?" *The New York Times*, December 12, 2004.

Kevin Carey,. "Point of View: Why Do You Think They're Called For-Profit Colleges?" *Chronicle of Higher Education*, July 30, 2010, A88.

"Community College Default Rate 16.7%," *The Des Moines Register via University Business*, January 4, 2010, http://www.universitybusiness.com/newssummary.aspx?news=yes&postid=21391.

Alan Contreras,). "Commentary: To Regulate For-Profit Colleges, Focus on What Matters," *Chronicle of Higher Education*, June 18, 2010, A29-30.

Sharona Coutts, "Investment Funds Stir Controversy Over Recruiting by For-Profit Colleges," *ProPublica*, July 9, 2010, http://www.propublica.org/article/investment-funds-stir-controversy-over-recruiting-by-for-profit-colleges.

"Daniels announces opportunity to increase access to higher education," *IN.gov*, June 11, 2010, http://www.in.gov/portal/news_events/54822.htm

"Data Points: A Snapshot of Recent Growth in Federal Student Loans," *Chronicle of Higher Education*, October 2, 2009.

Sam Dillon, "Troubles Grow for a University Built on Profits," *New York Times*, February 11, 2007, http://www.nytimes.com/2007/02/11/education/11phoenix.html.

John Dizard, "For-profit schools facing cuts," *Financial Times*, May 22, 2010.

Dick Durbin, "For-Profit Colleges and Federal Student Aid: Preventing Financial Abuses," (speech, National Press Club, June 30, 2010).

Jennifer Epstein, *Inside Higher Ed*: "Defining 'Gainful Employment,'" December 10, 2009; http://www.insidehighered.com/news/2009/12/10/employ; "Pushback on Gainful Employment," April 22, 2010, http://www.insidehighered.com/news/2010/04/22/gainful; "Partial 'Program Integrity,'" June 16, 2010, http://www.insidehighered.com/news/2010/06/16/regs; "Method to Miller's Madness," June 18, 2010, http://www.insidehighered.com/news/2010/06/18/credithour; "'Bad Apples' or Something More?" June 24, 2010, http://www.insidehighered.com/news/2010/06/24/forprofit; "The Senate Scrutiny Begins," June 25, 2010, http://www.insidehighered.com/news/2010/06/25/hearing; "Does the Messenger Matter?" July 15, 2010, http://www.insidehighered.com/news/2010/07/15/shorts; "Splitting the Difference on Gainful Employment," July 23, 2010, http://www.insidehighered.com/news/2010/07/23/gainful; "Closer Look at 'Gainful Employment,'" July 26, 2010, http://www.insidehighered.com/news/2010/07/26/regs; "Congress's 'Secret Shopper,'" August 3, 2010, http://www.insidehighered.com/news/2010/08/03/gao; "Shellacking the For-Profits," August 5, 2010, http://www.insidehighered.com/news/2010/08/05/hearing; "Has the Conversation Changed?" August 9, 2010, http://www.insidehighered.com/news/2010/08/09/forprofit; "What Harkin Wants," August 10, 2010, http://www.insidehighered.com/news/2010/08/10/forprofit; and "Phoenix Pays to Tell Its Story," September 1, 2010, http://www.insidehighered.com/news/2010/09/01/phoenix.

Jennifer Epstein and Doug Lederman, "Colleges Weigh In on Rules," *Inside Higher Ed,* August 4, 2010, http://www.insidehighered.com/news/2010/08/04/comments.

Kelly Field, "Government Vastly Undercounts Defaults," *Chronicle of Higher Education*, June 11, 2010, http://chronicle.com/article/Many-More-Students-Are/66223/.

"For-Profit Colleges Take an Unwanted Turn in the Spotlight," *Chronicle of Higher Education*, July 2, 2010.

Daniel Golden, "Your Taxes Support For-Profits as They Buy Colleges," *Bloomberg BusinessWeek*, March 4, 2010, http://www.businessweek.com/news/2010-03-04/your-taxes-supporting-for-profit-firms-as-they-acquire-colleges.html.

Jennifer Gonzalez, "For-Profit Colleges, Growing Fast, Say They Are Key to Obama's Degree Goals," *Chronicle of Higher Education*, November 13, 2009, A17-18.

Anne Gross, *Spotlight Focuses on For-Profit Sector*, (NACUBO: National Association of College and University Business Officers, July 1, 2010, http://www.nacubo.org/Initiatives/Legislation/Legislative_Updates/Spotlight_Focuses_on_For-Profit_Sector.html).

Tom Harkin, *Emerging Risk: An Overview of Growth, Spending, Student Debt and Unanswered Questions in For-Profit Higher Education* (United States Senate Health, Education, Labor and Pensions Committee, June 24, 2010, http://help.senate.gov/newsroom/press/release/?id=2a870217-b476-492b-aace-d015d22bd13d&groups=Chair).

*How America Pays for College 2010* (national study, Sallie Mae Inc. and Gallup, August 2010, https://www.salliemae.com/about/news_info/research/how_america_pays_2010/).

Scott Jaschik, *Inside Higher Ed*: "Online Enrollment Up 17%," January 27, 2010, http://www.insidehighered.com/news/2010/01/27/online; "Another College is Sold to a For-Profit," May 24, 2010, http://www.insidehighered.com/news/2010/05/24/lambuth; and "Standing Up to 'Accreditation Shopping,'" July 1, 2010, http://www.insidehighered.com/news/2010/07/01/hlc.

Anaya Kamenetz, "Not Quite Ready for the Honor Roll" and "Universities Inc.," *Fast Company*, December 2009.

Kevin Kinser, *From Main Street to Wall Street: The Transformation of For-Profit Higher Education* (ASHE Higher Education Report, Volume 31, Number 5, New Jersey: Jossey-Bass / Wiley Periodicals, 2006, print).

Rebecca Knight, "Apollo shakes off critics as it plans UK push," *Financial Times*, April 5, 2010.

Melissa Korn, "US to Scrutinize For-Profit Career Colleges," *Wall Street Journal*, July 23, 2010, http://online.wsj.com/article/SB10001424052748703467304575383592380129362.html.

Gregory D. Kutz, "For-Profit Colleges: Undercover Testing Finds Colleges Encouraged Fraud and Engaged in Deceptive and Questionable Marketing Practices," (testimony before the US Senate Committee on Health, Education, Labor, and Pensions, United States Government Accountability Office, GAO-10-948T, August 4, 2010, http://www.eric.ed.gov/ERICWebPortal/search/detailmini.jsp?_nfpb=true&_&ERICExtSearch_Value_0=ED511120&ERICEExtSearchType_0=no&accno=ED511120

Michael Learmonth, "What Big Brands Are Spending on Google," *Advertising Age*, September 6, 2010, http://adage.com/digital/article?article_id=145720.

Doug Lederman, *Inside Higher Ed*: "Jury Orders U. of Phoenix Parent to Pay $277 million," January 17, 2008, http://www.insidehighered.com/news/2008/01/17/apollo; "$78.5M Settles U.

of Phoenix Case," December 15, 2009, http://
www.insidehighered.com/news/2009/12/15/apollo; "For-Profit Colleges Boom," April 7, 2010,). http://www.insidehighered.com/news/
2010/04/07/enroll; "No Letup from Washington," April 13, 2010, http://www.insidehighered.com/news/2010/04/13/hlc; "Comparing Higher
Ed to Wall Street," April 29, 2010, http://www.insidehighered.com/
news/2010/04/29/shireman; and "Damaging Data on Loan Repayment," August 16, 2010, http://www.insidehighered.com/news/2010/08/
16/eddata

Tamar Lewin, *New York Times*: "Facing Cuts in Federal Aid, For-Profit Colleges Are in a Fight," June 5, 2010, http://www.nytimes.com/
2010/06/06/education/06gain.html; and "For-Profit Colleges Mislead
Students, Report Finds," August 3, 2010, http://www.nytimes.com/
2010/08/04/education/04education.html.

Sara Lipka, "Academic Credit: A Currency with No Set Value,"
*Chronicle of Higher Education*, October 22, 2010, http://
chronicle.com/article/Academic-Credit-Colleges/124973/.

Mary Beth Marklein, "Plan cracks down on for-profit colleges," *USA
Today*, July 23, 2010.

"Monsters in the making? Washington grapples with a booming education industry," *The Economist*, July 24, 2010.

Gretchen Morgenson, "For-Profit Schools, Tested Again," *New York
Times*, October 30, 2010, http://www.nytimes.com/2010/10/31/
business/31gret.html.

"New Rules for Colleges on Defaults," *Associated Press via The New
York Times*, December 13, 2009, http://www.nytimes.com/2009/12/
14/education/14default.html.

"Quick Takes," *Inside Higher Ed*, June 22, 2010, http://
www.insidehighered.com/news/2010/06/22/qt.

Whitney Tilson and John Heins, "Discovering Value: Skip School Stocks," *Kiplinger's Personal Finance*, December 2010.

Kimberly Tuby and Amanda Ealla, *Scrutiny of For-Profit Universities May Signal Opportunity for Some Traditional Colleges, but Higher Regulatory Costs for All* (Moody's Investors Service, Report Number 126940, August 9, 2010).

"The Chronicle: Daily News: 10/01/2004–01," *Chronicle of Higher Education, email newsletter by Chronicle Reporting*, October 1, 2004.

Robin Wilson, "For-Profit Colleges Change Higher Education's Landscape," *Chronicle of Higher Education*, February 12, 2010, A1&16-19.

## WAITING FOR GODOT BIBLIOGRAPHY

Nanette Asimov, "Californians Think Highly of College, but not Funding, *San Francisco Chronicle*, November 12, 2009.

Warren Bennis and C.L. Max Nikias, "Don't let Cold Cost-Cutting Endanger the American Model of Higher Education," *Chronicle of Higher Education*, September 11, 2009.

Anne Carey and Karl Gelles, "How to Understand $12 Trillion Debt," *USA Today*, February 3, 2010.

Michael Crow, *Toward Institutional Innovation* (Association of Governing Boards of Colleges and Universities: Trusteeship, May 2010, http://www.agb.org/trusteeship/2010/mayjune/toward-institutional-innovation-america%E2%80%99s-colleges-and-universities).

Thomas Donlan, Editorial, *Barron's,* January 28, 2010.

Richard Ekman, "Preventing Doomsayers from Shaping the Debate,"

*Independent*, Fall 2009.

Karin Fischer and Beth McMurtrie, "India's Education Minister Seeks Stronger Ties with American Universities," *Chronicle of Higher Education*, November 13, 2009, A24-25.

John Fritze, "Bad Deal or Only Chance," *USA Today,* December 17, 2010.

Will Hoover, "UH, Faculty Union Reach Deal," *Honolulu Advertiser*, January 18, 2010.

Daniel Hurley, "State Outlook," *AASCU*, January 13, 2010.

Scott Jascik, "Waiting for Recovery," *Inside Higher Ed*, May 4, 2010.

Doug Lederman, "Stop Asking For Money," *Inside Higher Education*, December 7, 2009.

Carolyn Lockhead, "Stimulus Money Drying Up," *San Francisco Chronicle,* June 8, 2010.

"Quick Takes," *Inside Higher Ed*, December 8, 2010, http://www.insidehighered.com/news/2010/12/08/qt.

Anne Ryman, "Three Universities Seek Tuition Hikes of 16-31%," *Arizona Republic*, February 20, 2010.

Grant Sabather, *The College of 2020 Students*, (Chronicle Research Services, June2009).

Jeffery Sachs, "How to Tame the Budget Deficit," *TIME*, February 4, 2010.

Michael Scherer, "Recovery Insurance," *TIME*, December 21, 2009.

Gene Steoele, "The U.S. is Broke," *USA Today*, January 27, 2010.

Jim Toedtman, "Too Much Red Ink," *AARP Bulletin*, June 1, 2010, http://www.aarp.org/work/social-security/info-062010/too_much_red_ink.html.

Fareed Zakaria, "The Last Chance," *TIME*, November 29, 2010.


GENERATIONAL BARBELLS BIBLIOGRAPHY

Sandra Block, *USA Today*: "For many today, golden years mean less travel, more work,", July 1, 2008, A1&5; and "Layoffs raise Social Security questions for older workers," October 9, 2009, http://www.usatoday.com/money/perfi/retirement/2009-10-08-older-workers-layoffs-social-security_N.htm.

Mark Calvey, "Schwab warns against plundering retirement funds," *San Francisco Business Times*, September 11, 2009, http://sanfrancisco.bizjournals.com/sanfrancisco/stories/2009/09/14/newscolumn2.html.

Dennis Cauchon, *USA Today*: "Income of Young in 8-Year Nose Dive," September 18, 2005; and "American Workforce Growing Grayer," December 15, 2010.

Dennis Cauchon and Richard Wolf, "Census: Income fell sharply last year," *USA Today*, September 11, 2009, http://www.usatoday.com/news/washington/2009-09-10-census-healthcare_N.htm.

Marc. Freedman, *Encore* (New York, New York: Public Affairs Press, 2007).

Nancy Gibbs, "Generation Next," *TIME*, March 22, 2010.

Neil Howe and William Strauss, "The Next 20 Years—How Customer and Workforce Attitudes will Evolve," *Harvard Business Review*, July-August 2007.

Sharon Jayson, "'iGeneration' has no off-switch," *USA Today*, February 10, 2010, D1-2.

Anya Kamenetz, *Generation Debt: How Our Future was Sold Out for Student Loans, Credit Cards, Bad Jobs, No Benefits, and Tax Cuts for Rich Geezers—and How to Fight Back* (New York, New York: Penguin Group, Inc., 2007).

Joel Kotkin, "400 Million People Can't Be Wrong," *Newsweek*, April 16, 2010.

Luke Mullins, "Social Security's Wheel of Fortune," *US News & World Report*, October 2009.

Rick Newman, "Getting Real about Retirement," *US News & World Report*, October 2009.

Susan Mitchell, *American Generations: Who They Are and How They Live* (fifth ed., New Strategist Publications, 2005).

Diana Oblinger, *Understanding the New Students* (Educause, 2003).

Lynn O'Shaughnessy, "Debt-squeezed Gen X saves little," *USA Today*, May 20, 2008, B1-2.

*How Young People View Their Lives, Futures, and Politics* (Pew Research Center, January 9, 2007).

Robert Half, *Workplace Redefined: Shifting Generational Attitudes During Economic Change* (2010, http://www.roberthalf.us/ WorkplaceRedefined).

LESSONS FROM "OVER THERE" BIBLIOGRAPHY

Phil Baty, "Western dominance of education under threat," *Times*

*Higher Education Supplement*, August 27, 2009.

"Building America's competitiveness: Examining what is needed to compete in a global economy" (hearing before the Committee on Education and the Workforce, House of Representatives, 109th Cong. 1, 2006).

Joshua Cooper Ramo, "How to Think about China," *TIME*, April 19, 2010.

John Aubrey Douglass and Richard Edelstein, *The Global Competition for Talent* (Center for Studies in Higher Education, University of California Berkeley, October 2009, http://cshe.berkeley.edu/).

John Aubrey Douglass, Irwin Feller and C. Judson King, eds., *Globalization's Muse: Universities and Higher Education Systems in a Changing World* (Berkeley, California: Berkeley Public Policy Press, 2009).

Karin Fischer, "America Falling: Longtime Dominance in Education Erodes," *Chronicle of Higher Education*, October 9, 2009, A1&21-23.

Karin Fischer and Ian Wilhelm, "American Model of Higher Education May Need an Upgrade to Go Global," *Chronicle of Higher Education*, July 2, 2010.

Karin Fischer and Beth McMurtrie, "India's Education Minister Seeks Stronger Ties with American Universities," *Chronicle of Higher Education*, November 13, 2009, A24-25.

Paul L. Gaston, *The Challenge of Bologna: What United States Higher Education Has to Learn from Europe, and Why It Matters that We Learn It* (Sterling, Virginia: Stylus Publishing, 2010).

Mara Hvistendahl, *Chronicle of Higher Education*: "Asia Rising: Countries Funnel Billions into Universities," October 9, 2009, A1&25-

29; and "What the Shakeup in China's Education Ministry Could Mean for Reform," November 13, 2009, A24.

Aisha Labi, *Chronicle of Higher Education*: "Germany Encourages Partnerships in Research, March 5, 2010, A38; and "As Cuts Hit European Higher Education Hard," December 17, 2010.

Melinda Liu, "Shanghai Surprise," *Newsweek,* April 22, 2010.

Marion Lloyd, "Latin America Hopes to Lift Global Profile," *Chronicle of Higher Education*, April 23, 2010, A1&26-28.

Ashley Marchand, "More Students are Enrolling but Graduation Rates Stayed the Same," *Chronicle of Higher Education,* April 16, 2010.

Simon Marginson, "The Rise of the Global University," *Chronicle of Higher Education*, January 4, 2010.

Dana Mattioli, "With Fewer Opportunities, Home Looks Appealing," *Wall Street Journal,* December 15, 2009.

Joe McDonald, "China Set to Become Second Largest Economy," *San Francisco Chronicle,* August 20, 2010.

*Measuring Up 2008* (National Center for Public Policy and Higher Education, National Press Club, 2008).

Shailaja Neelakantan, "Industrialists Create New Private Universities in India," *Chronicle of Higher Education*, March 5, 2010, A35-37.

James G. Neuger and Jonathan Stearns, "EU nations approve $60 billion bailout for strapped Greece," *San Francisco Chronicle*, April 12, 2010, D3.

*QS World University Rankings 2010* (Quacquarelli Symonds, Ltd., 2010, http://www.topuniversities.com/university-rankings/world-university-rankings/2010/results).

Kevin Rowling, "Three-Year Degrees Including Bologna and India," *World Education Services*, February 25, 2010.

Klaus Schwab,, ed., *The Global Competitiveness Report 2009-2010* (Geneva, Switzerland: World Economic Forum, 2009).

Oliver Staley, "China Surpasses India in Sending Students to US," *Bloomberg*, November 15, 2010, http://www.bloomberg.com/news/2010-11-15/china-tops-india-for-most-international-students-studying-in-u-s-colleges.html.

Elizabeth Stanton, "Stocks flounder amid Euro concerns," *San Francisco Chronicle*, May 15, 2010, D2.

Rob Stein, "America Loses Its Stature as Tallest Country," *Washington Post*, August 13, 2007, http://www.washingtonpost.com/wp-dyn/content/article/2007/08/12/AR2007081200809.html.

Deborah Stine, *America Competes Act* (Congressional Research Service, June 30, 2009).

Ben Wildavsky, "The New Global College Marketplace," *US News & World Report*, May 2010.

Ian Wilhelm, May 21, 2010, "Hong Kong Shares Its Plans to Become a Major Academic Hub," *Chronicle of Higher Education*, A22-23.

Fareed Zakaria, *The Post American World* (New York, New York: W.W. Norton & Co., 2008).

THE CALIFORNIA BELLWETHER BIBLIOGRAPHY

*Almanac Issue*, (*Chronicle of Higher Education*, August 28, 2010).

*An Uphill Battle for State Budgets* (National Council of State Legislatures, July 2010).

Nanette Asnimov, "CSU Ups Tuition by 5%—for Now," *San Francisco Chronicle*, June 19, 2010.

Jessica Bloch, "UM Students Voice Concerns about Likely Cuts," *Bangor Daily News*, March 30, 2010.

Wyatt Buchanan, "Crisis Blamed for Faulty Projections," *Chronicle of Higher Education*, January 10, 2010.

Wyatt Buchanan, "Poll: Cal down over finanaces again," *San Francisco Chronicle*, January 19, 2010.

*The Master Plan, and the Erosion of College Opportunity* (California Higher Education, the National Center for Public Policy and Higher Education February 2009).

Maureen Kavanaugh and Natalie Walsh, "Sorting out Prop 13's Impact on Education," *These Days on KPBS*, March 29, 2010, kpbs.org.

Jack Dolan, "State U's Tap Student Fee for Unintended Projects," *Los Angeles Times*. April 4, 2010.

Sara Hebel, "State Cuts are Pushing Public College into Peril," *Chronicle of Higher Educatio,* March 19, 2010.

Chip Johnson, "Cal Initiative Process has Gone Off-Course," *San Francisco Chronicle*, March 10, 2010.

Judy Keen, "States Braced to Tighten FY10 Belts," *USA Today,* January 5, 2010.

Josh Keller, "As Pension Costs Rise, Public Colleges Pay the Price," *Chronicle of Higher Education*, September 3, 2010.

Marisa Lagos, "Courts Add to Budget Woes," *San Francisco*

*Chronicle,* May 23, 2010.

Phillip Matier and Andrew Ross, "UC Berkeley to admit more out-of-state students," *San Francisco Chronicle*, October 26, 2009.

Heather Murtaugh, "College Talk Cuts, Taxes," *Daily Journal,* March 3, 2010.

Chris Rauban, "UCSF Considers Layoffs to Pace Its Budget," *San Francisco Business Times*, February 26, 2010.

Arnold Schwarzenegger, *California State of the State Address*, July 17, 2010.

Deborah Soloman, "Big Man on Campus," *New York Times*, February 17, 2010.

Peter Stokes, "From Suvival to Sustainability," Eduventures, January 10, 2010.

Jack Stripling, "Capital City Rumble," *Inside Higher Ed*, March 19, 2010.

David Von Drehle, *TIME*: "In the US, Crisis in the State Houses," January 17, 2010 and "The Broker States of America," January 28, 2010.

## AMERICA'S COLLEGE BIBLIOGRAPHY

Susan Aud, *The Condition of Education, 2010* (National Center for Education Statistics, US Department of Education, May 2010).

Paul Baskew, "Community Colleges in California Feed the Heart," *Chronicle of Higher Education*, May 9, 2008.

Jill Biden, "Community Colleges: Our Work Has Just Begin," *Chronicle of Higher Education*, April 3, 2010.

Bryan Cook and Natalie Pullaro, *College Graduation Rates* (American Council on Education, September 2010).

Abby Goodnough, "New Meaning for Night Class at Two-Year College," *New York Times,* April 29, 2009.

Eric Hoover, "Community Colleges Anticipate Boom in Baby-Boomer Students," *Chronicle of Higher Education*, April 17, 2009.

Scott Jaschik, *Inside Higher Ed*: "Defining the Enrollment Boom,".December 18, 2009 and "Moving the Needle," January 20, 2010.

David Moltz, *Inside Higher Ed*: "Community Colleges' Unfounded Mandate," January 16, 2010 and "California's Deal with Kaplan," May 26, 2010.

Christopher Mullin, *AACC Policy Brief:* "Community Colleges Enrollment Surge,"December 2009; "Rebalancing the Mission: The Community College Completion Challenge," June 2010; and "Just How Similar? Community Colleges and the For-Profit Sector," November 2010.

"New Tuition Challenges at Many US Private Univesities," Moody's Special Comment, *AACC Policy Brief*, October 2009.

Bob Sever, "Trends in College Pricing," *Stamats Quick Takes*, February 25, 2010.

## SKIING BAREFOOT BIBLIOGRAPHY

Patricia Barry, "A User's Guide to Health Can Reform," *AARP Bulletin*, March 16, 2010.

Jeffrey Brainard, "Support Staff Jobs Double in 20 Years," *Chronicle of Higher Education*, August 5, 2010.

Michael Bugeja, "The Elephant in the Room: curricula glut," *Chronicle of Higher Education*, April 2, 2010.

*The Bulletin of Higher Education Administration*, Issues: 11-9, 2009; 5-4, 2010; 7-7, 2010.

Dennis Cauchon, *USA Today*: "States Streamline Reorg Amid Fiscal Crisis," March 16, 2010, and "Private Wages No Match for Feds," August 10, 2010.

Jonathan R. Cole, "Powerhouses," *The Economist,* January 7, 2010.

Nicholas Confessore, "Major SUNY Donor Links an Even Bigger Gift to Flexibiliy on Setting Tuition," *New York Times*, July 12, 2010.

Steven Crow, "Reconsider the Credit Hour," *Inside Higher Ed*, January 22, 2010.

Paul Fain, *Chronicle of Higher Education*: "Cuts Intensify Identity Crisis for Washington's Flagship Campus," September 3, 2010 and "Why Deep Tuition Discounts May Not Spell Financial Doom," May 7, 2010.

Andrea Fuller, "A One-Year Associate Degree," *Chronicle of Higher Education,* April 30, 2010.

David Glenn, "The Canon of College Majors Persists Amid Calls for Change," *Chronicle of Higher Education*, September 4, 2009.

Brian Kelly, "Rethinking Retirement," *US News & World Report*, October 2009.

Doug Lederman, "The Completion Catastrophy," *Inside Higher Ed*, March 4, 2010.

Jamie Merisotis, "Embracing the big goal as a national imperative," (keynote, USC Center for Enrollment Research Policy and Practice, January 14, 2010.

Davide Moritz, "Picking up the Pace," *Inside Higher Ed*, July 6, 2010.

Mike Mullane, "How Sputnik Changed the World," *The Forum*, October 4, 2007.

Becky Pallack "A Sampling of National Media Coverage of Higher Education," *Arizona Daily Star*, December 12, 2009.

Lisa Rathke, "Agriculture College Sells Cow Heads to Cut Costs," *Associated Press*, July 12, 2010.

Bill Schackner, "PA State Universities Consider Eliminating Some Majors, " *Pittsburgh Post-Gazette*, February 22, 2010.

Jack Stripling, "Extra Nudge Into the Sunset," *Inside Higher Ed*, December 11, 2009.

Penelope Wang, "How the BA Got Cheaper," *Money*, December 2007.

TOUCHING THE THIRD RAIL BIBLIOGRAPHY

John Bound, *Increasing Time to Bacaulaureate Degree in the United States* (the National Bureau for Economic Research, April 201).

Dennis Cauchon, *USA Today*: "For Feds More Get G-Figure Salaries," December 11, 2009 and "It Pays to Work for Uncle Sam," March 5, 2010.

David Crave, "Pensions and Partying Like It's 1999," *San Francisco Chronicle*, January 15, 2010.

Editorial, *USA Today:* "States Come to Grips with Pricely Pension Promises," January 15, 2010; . "You Can't Cut the Deficit without Touching Benefits," January 25, 2010; and "Ugly Truth about State Pensions Begins to Emerge," May 3, 2010.

Jay Greene, *Administrative Bloat at American Universities* (the Goldwater Institute, August 2010.

Jay Greene, "Colleges Bloated Bureaucracy," *Baltimore Sun*, August 17, 2010.

Eric Kelderman, "Stimulus Money Helps Colleges Avoid Slashing Budgets Now, but Big Cuts May Loom," *Chronicle of Higher Education*, January 12, 2009.

Dunstan McNichol, "Public Employee $1 Trillion Pension Gap Projected," *San Francisco Chronicle,* August 22, 2010.

Andrew Ross, "More Real Estate Woes for CalPERS," *San Francisco Chronicle*, March 12, 2010.

*The Trillion Dollar Gap* (Pew Research Center, February 2010).

## THE THREE-YEAR PUBLIC OPTION BIBLIOGRAPHY

Carol Aslanian and Natalie Green Giles, *Trends in Adult Learning: A 2006 Snapshot* (Aslanian Group, 2006).

Sandy Baum, "Student Demographics: As Students Change, Colleges Must Follow," *Chronicle of Higher Education*, August 27, 2010.

Goldie Blumenstyk, "In a Time of Crisis, Colleges Ought to be Making History," *Chronicle of Higher Education*, May 1, 2009. Retrieved from http://chronicle.com/article/In-a-Time-of-Crisis-Colleges/14982.

Kevin Carey, "Point of View: Why Do You Think They're Called For-

Profit Colleges?" *Chronicle of Higher Education*, July 30, 2010, A88.

Sharon Silke Carty, "Tata Nano–world's cheapest car–gets price hike, *USA Today Drive On*, July 19, 2010, http://content.usatoday.com/ communities/driveon/post/2010/07/tata-nano—worlds-cheapest-car— —gets-price-hike/1.

"Daniels: Ind. Needs 3-Year College Degrees," *Indianapolis Star via University Business*, April 20, 2010, http:// www.universitybusiness.com/ newssummary.aspx?news=yes&postid=22486.

John Dizard, "For-profit schools facing cuts," *Financial Times*, May 22, 2010.

*Draft Report of the Advisory Committee on Higher Education Cost Efficiencies to the Texas Higher Education Coordinating Board* (Texas Higher Education Coordinating Board, July 21, 2010, http:// www.thecb.state.tx.us/index.cfm?ObjectID=9D89F7D3-F892-EEA0-D923B6D6D465D781.

Ronald G. Ehrenberg, "The Perfect Storm and the Privatization of Public Higher Education," *Change*, January 2006.

Jennifer Epstein, "Express Lane to a BA," *Inside Higher Ed*, March 11, 2010, http://www.insidehighered.com/news/2010/03/11/threeyears

Peter A. Facione, "Commentary: A Straight-Talk Survival Guide for Colleges," *Chronicle of Higher Education*, March 20, 2009, http:// chronicle.com/article/A-Straight-Talk-Survival-Guide/3268.

Kelly Field, "A Year of College for All: What the President's Plan Would Mean for the Country," *Chronicle of Higher Education*, May 22, 2009, http://chronicle.com/article/A-Year-of-College-for-All-/ 44386.

Joni E. Finney, "A Reset for Higher Education," *Chronicle of Higher*

*Education,* August 27, 2010, A6.

Karin Fischer and Marc Parry, "How Obama's $12-Billion Plan Could Change 2-Year Colleges," *Chronicle of Higher Education,* July 20, 2009.

Karin Fischer, "Students Flooded into US in 2008," *Chronicle of Higher Education,* November 20, 2009, A1&20-21.

Jennifer Gonzalez, "Connecting with Part-Timers is Key Challenge for Community Colleges, Survey Finds," *Chronicle of Higher Education,* November 20, 2009, A19.

Nikhil Gulati, "UPDATE: Tata Motors Raises Prices of Nano Minicar by 3%-4%," *Wall Street Journal,* July 16, 2010, http://online.wsj.com/article/BT-CO-20100716-706173.html.

Sara Hebel and Jeffrey J. Selingo, "Obama's Higher-Education Goal is Ambitious but Achievable, College Leaders Say," *Chronicle of Higher Education,* March 6, 2009, A21.

Eric Hoover, "Where Life Earns Credit: 'Prior Learning' Gets a Fresh Assessment," *Chronicle of Higher Education,* March 19, 2010, A23-24.

Scott Jaschik, *Inside Higher Ed*: "The 3-Year M.D.," March 25, 2010, http://www.insidehighered.com/news/2010/03/25/threeyear; "An Agenda for Graduate Education," April 29, 2010, http://www.insidehighered.com/news/2010/04/29/grad; and "3-Year Degrees? Not So Fast," June 3, 2010, http://www.insidehighered.com/news/2010/06/03/aacu

Michael Learmonth, "What Big Brands are Spending on Google," *Advertising Age,* September 6, 2010, http://adage.com/digital/article?article_id=145720.

Doug Lederman, *Inside Higher Ed*: "How to Do More with Less,"

November 24, 2009, http://www.insidehighered.com/news/2009/11/. lumina; "Slipping (Further) Off the Pedestal," February 17, 2010, http:// www.insidehighered.com/news/2010/02/17/squeeze; and "Damaging Data on Loan Repayment," August 16, 2010, http:// www.insidehighered.com/news/2010/08/16/eddata.

Tamar Lewin, "Student Loan Default Rate Is Continuing to Increase," *New York Times*, September 13, 2010, http://www.nytimes.com/2010/ 09/14/education/14colleges.html.

Melissa Ludwig, "Report: Shift colleges' focus," *San Antonio Express-News*, July 29, 2010, http://www.chron.com/disp/story.mpl/metropoli-tan/7131352.html.

Jamie P. Merisotis, "Embracing the Big Goal as a National Imperative," (opening keynote address, USC Center for Enrollment Research, Policy and Practice, January 14, 2010).

"Monsters in the making? Washington grapples with a booming educa-tion industry," *The Economist*, July 24, 2010).

Kimberly Palmer, "The Day the Spending Stopped: A new frugality could remake the US economy and American life," *US News & World Report*, August 2008.

*Penn Law and Wharton Create 3-Year JD/MBA Degree* (University of Pennsylvania Law School, September 10, 2008, http:// www.law.upenn.edu/blogs/news/archives/2008/09/ penn_law_and_wharton_create_3-.html.

Naomi Schaefer Riley, "Bookshelf: Reading, Writing, Radical Change," *Wall Street Journal*, August 31, 2010.

Sandra R. Sabo, "After a Pounding, New Grounding," *Business Officer*, July 2010.

ter: Declining by degree," *The Economist*, September

Oliver Staley, "China Surpasses India in Sending Students to US," *Bloomberg*, November 15, 2010, http://www.bloomberg.com/news/2010-11-15/china-tops-india-for-most-international-students-studying-in-u-s-colleges.html.

Jack Stripling, "As the Crow Flies," *Inside Higher Ed*, July 16, 2010, http://www.insidehighered.com/news/2010/07/16/crow

"Student Loan Debt Clock Ticks Past $848 Billion," *Huffington Post*, August 31, 2010, http://www.huffingtonpost.com/2010/08/31/student-loan-debt-clock-t_n_700516.html.

L. Tamar, "Average College Debt Rose to $24,000 in 2009, Report Finds," *New York Times*, October 22, 2010, http://www.universitybusiness.com/newssummary.aspx.

"Tata Motors unveils the People's Car," (press release, Tata Motors Media Centre, January 10, 2008 http://www.tatamotors.com/our_world/press_releases.php?ID=340&action=Pull.

Pamela Tate, *Testimony on Higher Education in the United States and the Needs of Adult Learners: Recommendations for Strategic Directions* (Commission on the Future of Higher Education [Spellings Commission], January 31, 2006, http://www2.ed.gov/about/bdscomm/list/hiedfuture/1st-hearing/tate.pdf

Kimberly Tuby and Amanda Ealla, *Scrutiny of For-Profit Universities May Signal Opportunity for Some Traditional Colleges, but Higher Regulatory Costs for All* (Moody's Investors Service, Report Number 126940, August 9, 2010).

Martin Van Der Werf and Grant Sabatier, *The College of 2020: Students* (Chronicle Research Services, June 2009).

Ben Wildavsky, "University Globalization Is Here to Stay," *Chronicle of Higher Education*, August 27, 2010.

# Index

# ABOUT THE AUTHORS

**DAN ANGEL** is president of Golden Gate University in San Francisco. He has served as president of three community colleges (Texas and California), two public universities (Texas and West Virginia), and a private, nonprofit university (California). He was elected to three terms in the Michigan House of Representatives where he served on the College and University Committee and has also been a special assistant to US Senator Robert P. Griffin in Washington, DC. Angel has served on the Dallas Federal Reserve Board and was named Administrator of the Year in Austin, Texas, and Most Admired CEO in the category of "Turnaround" for the *San Francisco Business Times*. The author of a biography on former Michigan Governor George Romney, he has authored, co-authored, edited, or co-edited a dozen books.

**TERRY CONNELLY** is dean of the Ageno School of Business at Golden Gate University with thirty-five years of experience as a corporate lawyer with Cravath Swaine & Moore in New York and London; chief of staff of global investment banking at Salomon Brothers; head of global investment banking at Cowen & Company; and director of strategic services for Ernst & Young Australia. His commentaries on the mortgage and financial crisis and related regulation, national economic policy, and Federal Reserve actions have been quoted by the Associated Press, Reuters, CNN, CNBC, Business Week, and a broad range of national and regional media outlets, as well as in interviews with the BBC World Service and China International Radio. He is a Trustee of the Institute of Transpersonal Psychology in Palo Alto, California.

Made in the USA
Lexington, KY
13 September 2011